DARKBORN
THE MASTER MAGE CHRONICLES
BOOK ONE

HENRY JACOBSEN

Kinsley!

I hope you enjoy
the book!

Henry.

henry@hdjacobson.com

DEDICATION

This book and the others in this series are dedicated to my family. First, to my wife of five decades who challenged me on a cold and wintery Wyoming afternoon with the words:"Good grief! Go write a book!" And to my two wonderful children, Joshua and Jutta, who have always believed I could.

Appreciation and a sincere thank-you to friends and family who have read the manuscripts and offered encouragement and advice.

PROLOGUE

The lunar shadow streaked across the land. It began on the island kingdom of Iber, then swept across the Betting Sea to the mainland kingdoms of Caldonia, Suerca, Tumano and Adnium. It crossed mountain ranges, rivers, valleys and plains until finally disappearing over the western Illium desert.

In Alexa, capitol of Iber, High-mage Bekka lay in her final stages of labor. It had been a difficult pregnancy. And it was made worse by the sudden passing of her husband, High-mage Myron of Sage. He had fallen victim to a recurring plague that had swept the Kingdom the prior turn. She herself had been affected, but survived in a weakened condition.

"One more push, mi'lady. We're almost there," encouraged the healer-mage. "Just once more and it will all be over." At the darkest height of the lunar passing, when the gorge of *gift* reach its peak, a baby's cry was heard. "A boy! You have a son! *Fata* bless us all."

"May the *fata* bless us all indeed," muttered Lord High-mage Saul, the newborn's grandfather and advisor to Justin, his brother-by-marriage and current King of Iber. Saul gave a spontaneous shudder. *Why is it with this child I feel we will most certainly need all the help the* fata *can bestow?*

As always, the naming of the child fell to the family patriarch. Saul spoke firmly for all to hear: "His name shall be Marcus, Marcus Aurelius." *The ninth,* he whispered to himself, for none were to hear the last. "Dark-born and heir to the office of Lord High-mage to the King. May he be strong in both *gift* and wisdom." Then more unspoken words: *Especially in wisdom.* The naming ceremony was over and the babe was given to the health-mage, who in turn passed him to a wet nurse. The child cried briefly and fell silent.

That night, the rigors of delivery and disease took its toll. The mother, High-mage Bekka, lay dead.

CHAPTER

ONE

"Grandfather?"

"Yes, Marcus, you have a question?"

"Well, it was something we were taught today in school. What are the *fata*?"

"*Fata*?" Well, son, *fata* is old-speak for the *fates*. *Fatum, fata.* The *fata* control the destiny of all people, men and women alike."

"Our priest-mage said there were three."

"Yes, so we are taught.

"Are they people?"

"A good question, but one for which I have no answer. Some believe they are. But most say they are just natural laws. Either way, the three control our destiny. You were taught their names, yes?"

"Of course."

" Then let's discuss them. The first *fatum*, or *fate*, is judgment. It, we cannot escape. Eventually, and with certainty, it claims us all. The other two *fata* are justice and mercy. A fair judgment requires that 'justice be satisfied'. Would you not agree?"

"Yes, grandfather, I do. Otherwise, as you just said, it would not be fair."

"Indeed! Fortunately, justice can be tempered by mercy. But mercy cannot *rob* justice."

"What do you mean, 'mercy cannot rob justice'?"

Saul thought for a moment how to answer the boy's question. "Suppose you steal a gold crown from me. Justice says you must repay me, right?"

"Of course."

"But if I am merciful and forgive you the theft, I still suffer a one-crown loss, right?"

Marcus was slow to answer. "Well, yes."

"So has mercy robbed me of the crown I might otherwise regain through justice?"

Again Saul let Marcus ponder a reply. "It would, unless you were compensated in some other way."

Saul was pleased the boy reached this conclusion. He was but eight turns of age. "And what might be adequate compensation?"

"Well, perhaps I could find someone else to pay you the coin? Oh, but then I would just be in debt to the other person, instead of you. He paused again, thinking. "So, what is the answer?"

"The coin of mercy, my son. Everyone is in debt to another, or has caused injury in some way. If I am shown mercy, I repay the merciful by extending mercy to someone else. Do you not remember the eight virtues of the *fata*?"

"Yes. The priest-mage who taught made us memorize them. Two turns ago."

"And what are the first two?"

"Well, the first is 'respect the *fata* and swear not in their name'. And the second is 'deal justly with all, but extend mercy that you might receive mercy in return'. Oh, now I see what that means. Before now, it was just words."

"Return to your room and think about the other six virtues. They are words, yes. But words to live by. And remember this.

Judgment is a two-edged blade. It rewards the obedient as surely as it punishes those who are not."

Marcus lay in bed, pondering the other six virtues.

-- *Do not wantonly take the life of man or beast.*

-- *Follow virtue and fidelity all your days.*

-- *Steal not but be honest in all things.*

-- *Be generous to the poor and to those who serve the* fata.

-- *Protect the weak, especially the womb and cradle.*

-- *The seventh is a day of rest for both man and beast.*

The priest-mage had explained how each of these virtues affected his life and life of others. Grandfather was right. Following them would protect him, or anyone, from a harsh judgment. He fell into a peaceful sleep.

Marcus had reached a hand-age. As was the custom of Iber, the time had come for him to consider his intended path in life. But for Marcus, the path was pre-determined. He would follow in the family tradition of service to his grand-uncle, King Justin of Iber, and his successors. Such had been the case for countless generations past. His grandfather and guardian, Lord High-mage Saul, had carefully groomed his ward for such a life. The first five turns were of strict childhood discipline and attention to duty and respect. The child had been sheltered from the idleness and coarse influence of other children. In short, Marcus' childhood had been one of cheerless instruction and adherence to what his grandfather considered *appropriate royal behavior.*

Training for royal- and high-born youth followed several five-turn cycles. From birth to five, pre-school and discipline. From five to one-hand, literacy and basic academics. And from a hand to one-hand five, physical conditioning and pre-professional training. At that age, a young adult transitioned to a chosen profession and formally entered the workforce, usually as an apprentice or intern. For the very few, those with a strong endowment of *gift* and sufficient coin, there might be specialized training at a university. It would be for both safety and the profitable integration of *gift* into society. In any case, at the age of two-hands, a young man or woman was considered a full adult with all the rights and responsibilities thereof.

Marcus had been a good and diligent student. At the age of a hand he could read and write the kingdom's language of *Turga*. He understood numbers and sums and had a basic grasp of science and the arts. He also had a working knowledge of *Rontal*, the dialect of the mainland kingdoms. There was really little difference between the two. His training reflected the nature of his future service, established by a tradition of four-hand generations. Marcus understood he would succeed his grandfather and become the Lord High-mage. He would be advisor and protector of the current and future kings and queens of Iber. All that remained was the question of *gift*: which endowment he had been given and its power. How it would be developed. And how it would best contribute in his service to the royal family. It was possible he would be devoid of *gift*. This happened in generations past. If so, he would still become the advisor to the reigning monarch, but Lord High-*mage* in title only. *Gift* ran strongly in the Aurelius family line. But skipping generations was not uncommon. If so, it had not of great concern. Subsequent generations had held the title in a more complete way.

Gift was the extension of the natural force that gave life to all that lived. Withdrawal of all *gift* constituted death. There were some who possessed *gift* beyond that needed for life itself. Such individuals were considered *gifted*, and their additional *gift* was manifested in an endowment, or in some cases multiple endowments.

An endowment was the unique expression of one's *gift*. And

endowments came with great diversity of strength and nature. What determined its *power* was endlessly debated. Clearly, *gift* ran stronger in some family lines. So to a certain extent, it was inherited. But there were parents and children in traditionally *gifted* families that had no additional *gift* at all, or so very little as to be of no consequence. In the general public, the presence of a *gifted* individual was uncommon, bordering on rare. But occasionally one arose with remarkable strength.

Those particularly strong in *gift*, those who became mages or high-mages, were able to perform amazing and sometimes inexplicable feats with their *gift* power. There were simple things common to all mages, such as casting flame and creating light, or moving small objects without touch. Those particularly strong in such areas were considered to have the *earth-gift* endowment. Exceptional accountants and businessmen were said to have a *maths-* or *merchant-gift*. Extraordinary soldiers and leaders had *battle-gift*. Those having *scholar-gift* were marked by an aptitude and passion for study, including languages. These tended to the professions of *fata* priests, teachers, and researchers of all types. Others, artists and exceptional craftsmen, had the *artisan-gift*, and so on.

Some *gifts* were considered more useful than others. *Health-gift* was the most common and prized. *Earth-gift* and *artisan*-gift were valued for their utility in many practical aspects of life, particularly the manipulation of physical objects and materials. Of all the endowments, *mind-gift* was feared the most, for it gave the possessor a power to probe and influence the mind of others. Fortunately, it was very uncommon, and rarely strong.

Within royal and high-born families, where *gift* was common, endowments were highly esteemed and usually cultivated. Those with *gift* held certain advantages over those without. But the presence of *gift* was not given a high profile outside the family. It was suspicion and fear of *mind-gift* in particular that tainted all other forms of endowment, especially with the general public. For them, the only trusted *gift* was for healing. Why? Because it was frequently needed and often unassociated with other endowments and manifestations.

Saul's parents and his daughter had been strong in *gift*. He himself had *gift*, but with no great power in any particular area. He was mildly studious, but not exceptionally so. When younger, he frequented and enjoyed Iber's modest chapel, which held a number of manuscripts. It was a small collection, Saul knew, even *meager* compared to the truly great chapel libraries and university collections known to exist in the mainland kingdoms. Even many of their parish chapels, responsible for the teaching of children, were said to have more learning resources than what was available here in Iber. But the few documents here were old ones, some written in ancient *Kult* with references to the even older language of the *Elken*.

Kult, translated from *Elken*, was the language for accessing the powers of *gift*. It was believed that if one could understand and speak *Elken*, he (or she) would be able to access the legendary strength of *gift* used so powerfully in ancient times. But alas, *Elken* was a long-long-dead and lost language, and only scattered remnants of its strange written glyphs remained as passing references in the oldest of *Kult* manuscripts. And *Kult* itself was a dead, unspoken language, as well. Saul had heard rumors of a few old mages who claimed they could actually read and understand its odd characters. People like aged *Kentuck the Crazy*. Saul knew Kentuck and of his obsession for learning *Kult*, but doubted he was as fluent as some believed. Even if it were true that Kentuck could read *Kult*, it would do little to enhance the use of *gift*. It was one thing to know what the *Kult* characters meant, quite another to know how to pronounce them correctly.

The meager *gift* language that Saul knew and occasionally used, had passed from *Elken* to *Kult* to *Turga*, the common language of Iber. Mages on the mainland spoke the *Rontal* dialect, which was similar to *Turga*. One was considered to be a minor variation of the other. Saul had read that *Turga*, being an 'older' language (at least by some accounts) had retained a better translation from *Kult*. If so, perhaps the Iberian mages accessed *gift* more powerfully than their mainland counterparts? Saul suspected this was not true, but based primarily on simple Iberian pride. But then, such was hard to know, for Iber had infrequent interaction with the mainland kingdoms or their mages.

All of this passed through Saul's mind as he contemplated the forward path for the hand-old Marcus. The boy had shown an aptitude for study, so he would likely have success in languages, science and the arts. He was tall for his age and agile, which would allow him to pursue any number of physically demanding trades. But of course, none of this really mattered. Marcus would become a mage and advisor to the King and protector of the royal household. To do so he must learn to become a blades-man, just as he had. *Protect the royal family with blade as well as gift.* When the boy reached puberty, when *gift* traditionally emerged, perhaps other decisions could or would be made. For now, training in edged weapons was required.

CHAPTER
TWO

"OUCH." Marcus cradled his right hand, still holding a wooded long-blade, in his left. The blood from his bruised and bleeding knuckles seeped through his fingers.

Blade-master Kelson laughed. "Better bruised fingers now than missing fingers later! Again, you must hold the blade so that blows are deflected by the guard, away from the hand, when I move the way I did. You are allowing my blade to pass over the guard as you pivot to the right, as I have shown you time and time again."

"I will get, it Master Kelson. Really I will. Let's try it a few more times."

Kelson liked the boy. He was a fast learner and a willing student. The fact that Marcus once more had battered fingers was not a concern, nor was it surprising. He, Kelson, was a master blades-man, and was able to defeat or disarm virtually any opponent he faced. The fact that Marcus was only rarely taken in this way, at the age of one-hand two, was remarkable in its own right. Again they faced each other and again Kelson gave the feint left, then right, then left again. Same as before. But this time,

Marcus was ready. He ignored the feints and deflected Kelson's strike effectively, but then surprised him with a quick strike of his own, slapping him sharply on the blade arm.

"Ow! Huh? How were you able to do *that?*"

"Because you told me the move you were going to make. I don't think I would be so lucky in a real fight, right?" It was clear, though, that Marcus was pleased to get one over on his instructor.

Kelson laughed. "Perhaps yes, perhaps no. Either way, well done! Perhaps that's enough for today. I think I'll go and soak my arm. Here, put this away for me." He tossed Marcus the wooden training blade.

Marcus returned the practice blades to the rack on the pit wall and headed off to his next class. Kelson paused and turned in the direction of the castle. As expected, he found the Lord High-mage in his study. "Saul, we need to talk, my friend, about your grandson."

Saul looked up, startled. "What? Why? Has he been misbehaving in some way?"

"No, nothing of the sort. If anything, he's too polite, almost lacking in aggression, you know, that killer instinct it takes to be a truly great blades-man, or a blade-master."

"And is that so bad at the age of a hand and two? Surely a man of your violence can train that out of him!" Saul said. There was a hint of amusement in his voice. "And you have plenty of time to do so."

"Oh, of course, that's not a concern. But I came here to talk to you about *where* he is in his training. Today he caught me on the blade arm with a rather painful strike. "

"Sorry to hear of it. I would think that with your experience, a boy so young wouldn't be taking advantage of you in such a way. Are you getting old, slowing down? Huh?"

"Very funny, Saul. You know that isn't the case. It's just that I haven't had someone do that to me in a long time, a v-e-r-y long time. I've been wondering, have you ever thought about testing him for *gift*?"

"Kelson, my friend, he's a hand and two turns old. I hardly think he would be manifesting *gift* at this age. Perhaps he just has fast reflexes? Some children do, you know that. Take that little tow-headed pick-pocket down on market street."

"Saul, I have been a blade-master for over two-hand five turns. I know all about those 'fast reflexes' as you call them. Marcus is beyond fast reflexes. It's as though he reads my mind and knows what my next moves are going to be. Again I ask you, have you thought about testing him for *gift*? And how much mind-*gift* and battle-*gift* do you have in your family lines?"

"Mind-*gift*, yes, but nothing strong. Battle-*gift*? In our line? Not much that I recall. In fact, none for all I know. Nevertheless, you and I both know that endowments in *gift* are granted as the *fata* will. But no. No history of battle-mages in our line that I know of. I still think you're making something out of nothing."

Kelson nodded a polite good-bye and left, leaving Saul pondering the request. Have Marcus tested for *gift*? It was simple enough to do, but not without risk. On the positive side, knowing that Marcus has *gift* at this early age would allow Saul to direct his development that much sooner. But this was out-weighed by the negatives. *If* Marcus were to have *gift* at the tender age of hand-and-two, it would mean that *gift* had emerged before his transition to manhood. And if that were true, he would be exceptionally *gifted*, even extraordinarily so. And if he were perceived as a powerful mage-to-be, life would be difficult. Powerful mages of any age were feared more than trusted. And more often than not, such fear turned to hate, and hate to violence. Not a good situation for any man, let alone a boy. And further, once an emerging mage were introduced to the powers of *gift*, it would be like opening the gates of a great dam. A flood of more and greater *gift* would soon follow, to unknown consequences for one so young. These were burdens he would not wish on the boy, not yet. Not at the age of a hand and two.

As the Lord High-mage to the King, Saul (and therefore Marcus) ate consistently well. The evening venison was nicely spiced, the vegetables and tubers plentiful and tender. With a contented sigh, Saul pushed himself from the small table and turned his attention to Marcus. "So, Kelson came and told me you bested him today, gave him a right smack across the blade arm. He was quite impressed."

Marcus laughed. "He invited me to do it, told me exactly where his arms would be, and when. And I could hardly pass up the opportunity, for all the times he's struck me!"

Saul laughed as well. He called for the serving maid. She came quickly and cleared away the dishes and remaining food. "We, meaning you and I, have a little activity tonight. One you might find entertaining."

Marcus raised his eyebrows in interest. "Sounds fun. Something new?"

"Hmm. I certainly hope so."

For all the negatives associated with the test for *gift*, one thing overcame them all: Saul's compulsive curiosity. The likelihood of *gift* emergence at the age of hand and two was not unheard of, but only with youth who had matured at a very young age. Marcus, though large for his age, was still a boy. If indeed he had emerged, it would be a rare event to be studied closely. Saul simply had to know.

Though they lived in the royal palace, their accommodations were modest: a common room with several comfortable chairs and a somewhat worn sofa, two bedrooms, one larger than the other, a small kitchen and eating area, and a relieving room with a toilet and brass tub.

Saul and Marcus retired to the common room. It was late in the turn, so the meager light through the arrow-slit windows left the room in deep shadow. The flame in the pit had not been lit, making the room cool as well as dark.

"The time has come, Marcus, to talk somewhat about *gift*. What do you know? What have you been taught?"

"Well," began Marcus. "You have told me it is that which gives life, and that all living things have it. Right?"

"Yes. Without *gift* there is no life. And if *gift* is withdrawn from a living thing, it dies. *Gift* then goes back to the earth from which it came. For a few, for a *very* few, *gift* is given in much greater abundance. This gives them advantages over those without. Their extra *gift* can be manifested and used in many ways. This is called their *endowment* in *gift*."

"Like healing? What health-mages sometime do?"

"Yes, that is a well-known example. But there are many more. So many, in fact, that no one knows all the ways *gift* expresses itself. Suffice it to say, *gift* and its endowments are unique to each individual, so no two people strong in *gift*, have the same strengths and weaknesses in their ability to use it.

"What makes one mage's *gift* different from another's *gift*. And why do a few have it but most do not?"

"Ah. Good questions, my lad. For which I have no sure answer. Clearly, some families tend to be stronger than others. Our line of strong mages goes back many generations." *At least four-hands, Saul thought to himself.* "I believe it also depends a bit on where and when you are born. Most mages come from cities, rather than rural areas. I'm not absolutely sure why, though I have my suspicions. But enough questions. Tonight I want to see if you have been blessed with *gift* of your own. Kelson thought you were too quick for your age and training, and raised the question to me this post mid-day."

"So grandfather, how do you test for *gift*? Is it something like I do in my classes, the question and answer thing? If so, I'm sure I don't, because you have already heard me tell you all I know about it."

"No. A test for *gift* is something much more practical. It's something you *do*. I will tell you how to access *gift*. You are either able to do what I instruct you to do, or not. Either way is acceptable. If you don't have *gift* now – and it is highly unlikely that you do at your age – that does not mean you won't have access to it when you are a bit older. In all of the cases I know, *gift* doesn't manifest itself until you go through the change to become a young man."

"I understand. What do you want me to do?"

"First, you need to know the correct words to use. Some manifestations of *gift* only respond to ancient words of power. Such words that have to be spoken clearly and precisely. If words are said poorly, *gift* will respond very weakly. Or probably not at all. Now, I'm going to teach you the word for flame. This is a simple and practical use of *gift*, and is usually the first application taught to those who are *gifted*. It's f-o-t-i-a. But you must pronounce it foe-see-AH. If you pronounce it FO-she-ah or fo-SHE-ah, as most mages are taught, you can still cast flame, but it will be very weak. So, try it. Remember: fo-see-AH."

"Fo-see-AH. Fo-see-AH. Fo-see-AH. Does that sound right? Is that all there is to it?"

Saul laughed. "To answer your two questions: Yes. No. Yes, it sounds correct. No, that is not all there is to invoke flame. You must *cast* the words and at the same time, draw *gift* from your own reservoir of life force to send it forth. That is why so few people can use *gift* to do anything useful, They only possess sufficient life force to stay alive. If a person does not have additional *gift*, say, to create flame, no amount of training can help. They cannot access power that is not naturally within them. Now, I want you to try to cast a small flame into our burn-pit. This is how. First, you must imagine in your mind, what that flame should look like: blazing logs, hot coals. I'm sure you know exactly how that looks. Then I want you to raise your hands, or maybe just your right hand, and *cast* that image into the burn-pit, at the same time saying foe-see-AH. Now, try it. Think of blazing logs in the burn-pit."

Marcus stood quietly for a several long breaths, then raised his right hand high over his head. "Fo-see-AH" he shouted, flinging his hand toward the burn-pit.

The wood in the pit exploded in a burst of sparks and billowing smoke. In an instant, both Saul and he were struggling for breath, stomping out embers throughout the room. Ash was falling everywhere and into everything.

"Well, that was interesting. It appears you have the flame thing mastered. Maybe next time, you won't need to shout so loudly."

Marcus sat silently, eyes drooping. "I... I don't feel so good. Like I want to go and lay down. I don't know if I like this *gift* stuff so much."

Saul nodded, pensively. The child had accessed *gift* in an extraordinary way. But he had no deep reservoir, yet. Using even such a small amount had draw from his life force. To call forth flame again, without adequate rest, would leave him weaker still. There would be no more testing for now, and probably not for quite some time. And there was no point in doing so. The question of *gift* had been asked and most conclusively answered.

Marcus slept deeply the night after testing. He awoke briefly for a breakfast of flat-bread, eggs and tea. He then returned to his bed. He arose again for supper, then returned to his bed and slept again through the night. On the second day he arose with much of his normal vigor. Marcus found his grandfather in his offices, deep in thought.

"I am sorry, my son, for hurting you so."

"What do you mean, 'hurting me'?" asked Marcus.

"I didn't realize, I didn't anticipate, what could happen when I asked you to cast flame. I endangered your life, and I am sorry for that."

"Well, for what it's worth, it was a bit of surprise for me, too," Marcus responded, a bit of humor in his voice. "Does this mean that I have *gift* and might someday become a mage like you?"

"Again, you ask two questions, not just one. Such impatience! To answer your *questions*: Yes. No. Yes, you have *gift*, and no, you will not be a mage such as I."

The boy's face dropped in disappointment. "All I have ever wanted has been to be like you, grandfather. And you say I cannot?"

"Ah, but you didn't let me finish. You will not be what I am, because I believe you will be much *more* than what I am. At the age of a hand-and-two, you have already accessed *gift* more powerfully than most adults. Could I have done what you did two nights ago? Yes. But I have grown in *gift-strength* for over sixty turns." Saul paused and chose his next words carefully. "And herein is the problem, Marcus. I fear that you might become *too* strong in *gift*, and it could lead to a very troubled life indeed, possibly even to your death."

Marcus raised his eyes to look into those of his grandfather. "Why... why would you say something like that? Did I... did I do something terribly wrong in casting flame? Isn't that exactly what you asked me to do?"

Saul sighed. *How to explain this in some simple way that Marcus would understand.* "Once upon a time there was a man who bought a puppy. It was a big puppy, the largest of its litter. Over time, the dog grew and grew and grew. It was a gentle dog, but people began to fear its size and strength. They demanded the owner do away with the dog, lest it rise up and bite them. When he refused, the village folk came and took the dog away. Do I need to complete the story?"

Marcus' face fell. "No, I understand. You believe I am going to become strong in *gift* and will become that 'big dog' of which you spoke. And if people know that I am a 'big dog', or might become one, they will feel threatened and will want to do away with me, even if I do nothing to make them afraid."

"Yes, son, that is so. Why? Because sometime in the past there *was* a big dog that became dangerous. They will fear you, not for what you are, but for what you might become."

"I understand that, grandfather. But what does that mean for me? Can I get rid of my *gift*? Can I hide it? Can I just run away?"

"Again, three questions, not just one. No. Yes. Yes. You cannot avoid the powers of *gift*, especially now that they have been opened. Your power in *gift* will grow, whether you wish it to or not, according to your natural endowment. The best you can do is to learn to live with it in a way that is both safe and constructive. And may I say, that is easier said than done, and best done under the supervision of stronger mages. As to hiding your power in *gift*, I said 'yes' because to a large extent you can. Your use of *gift* is mostly a conscious act that you initiate. If you can discipline yourself to *never* access *gift*, or use it discretely, you can go undetected, to a degree. But as your power grows, this will become more and more difficult. Why? Because there are mages who can detect the presence of your *gift* whether you use it or not. Your third question was one of simply running away. I think you know the answer to that one. You can run away from people, from those who would do you harm. But your *gift* will always follow. So running would only be effective for a time. There is, of course, a fourth path."

Marcus had been listening carefully. Very carefully. "And what would that be?"

"You must become so powerful that you are beyond the threat of others. But, sadly, that has never worked, as far as I know."

They sat quietly for a time.

"So, what next, grandfather."

"Choice number two: hide your *gift-power*. We will work together to develop your *gift*-strength, but it must be hidden at all cost. This means *never* mentioning it, to *anyone*. Not to Kelson. Not to your cousin, the prince – *especially* not to him -- nor *any* of the royal family. They would be the first to feel threatened by your power. Never even to friends. And never, never access your *gift* except under my supervision. I am afraid you are destined for a lonely, solitary life. I wish there were another way."

"I understand. And you are right, this is going to be difficult."

Marcus had felt a door open to an influx of *gift-power* after his testing. The testing itself had left him drained of energy. Saul had called it an "over-casting" of *gift*, a form of *gift sickness*. And had reassured him that no lasting harm had been done and its effects would quickly pass. But with it came a warning. 'A deeper cast of *gift* could withdraw enough life-force to create disability, even death.' As predicted, it took several days to recover. There were no lasting effects. Rather, Marcus felt a subtle increase in vigor and stamina. And his senses had sharpened.

Saul repeatedly warned Marcus to avoid any display of *gift*. When Kelson had asked if he had been tested, Marcus had given an oblique reply. 'Yes, but it did not go as intended.' When Kelson inquired further, Marcus had simply said, 'I think we expected a mild positive response. But like I said, it just didn't go as expected.' A half-truth it was, but it seemed to satisfy Kelson's curiosity at the time. Strangely, Saul seemed to lose interest in any further testing or training in *gift* with him. This left him quite frustrated, as his curiosity, now aroused, dominated his idle thoughts. So, heeding Saul's warning on over-casting, Marcus began to experiment. The only 'words of power' he knew were for casting flame – foe-see-AH – and for casting light, lu-see-AH. As for flame, he found that if he spoke in the lowest of whispers, and cast with a minimum of intensity, he could safely ignite a candle. And it seemed to have no physical effect on him in doing so. Casting light was even less taxing. And he discovered, to his fascination, that he did not even need to speak the words of power. He could mentally invoke *focia* and cast it to ignite the candle. He had to focus intently on the wick, however, before doing so.

Marcus suspected that some aspects of the *gift* endowment he possessed were natural to him and did not require any 'words of power'. In the case of mind-touch, it was just *there*. It was *always* present. And as such, it was hard to hide and even harder to ignore. And what was this *mind-touch*? Marcus had discovered, somewhat by accident, that he could use *gift* to lightly reach into an opponent's mind, listen, and thus anticipate his next move. It was somewhat like the endowment of *mind-power* his grandfather had described, except he was *pulling* thoughts rather than *casting* them. As such, his opponents had no idea whatsoever they were being compromised. Within a turning, it gave him an unassailable advantage in combat.

Marcus had used it so often that it was now second nature to him, and he did it without conscious effort. It required virtually no *gift* power on his part. The real challenge had been combat with the really accomplished blades-men, like blade-master Kelson. They acted and reacted by instinct, reflexes honed by turns and turns of practice. Marcus began prevailing against them, but not without intense focus. Any slip in position or form would inevitably result in defeat. And he was loathe to lose.

Marcus let his opponent feint left, knowing that he would follow up with a blade-thrust to the right. He deflected the blow and returned to a neutral position. As usual, this training round would end in a frustrating draw and an exhausted foe. Marcus would not be wearied. Defense was much less taxing than offense.

Remembering Saul's admonition to maintain a low profile in such matters, Marcus had adopted a practice of avoiding the inevitable notoriety of a *prodigy* blades-man. If he were to win-win-win, everyone would notice and he would become a celebrity opponent. He would attract observers at every turn, and blades-men would vie for the opportunity to confront him. But losing was not an appealing alternative. So he adopted a "no-win" strategy: spar until his exhausted adversary conceded to a draw. It was frustrating to fight against, boring to watch. Before long Marcus had achieved his goal: anonymity. And the process of constantly reading opponents and reacting defensively was instructive. He had become ever more proficient in the principles of blade-work. And in physical strength. He had (with permission) taken a practice long-blade to his quarters. Once Saul had retired for the night, Marcus would endlessly practice the moves he had been shown that day. Kelson had taught that practice did not make perfect. 'Practice makes permanent. If you practice poor form, the weakness will follow you forever.' So Marcus was careful to follow the new moves with absolute attention to detail. Kelson: 'It is *perfect* practice, that creates perfect performance.'

THREE

I t had been two turnings since he had tested Marcus for *gift*. Everything had been quiet for Saul, except for the arrival of a new and additional *advisor mage* to King Justin. His name was Sinifir, and there was something *off-putting* about the man, though Saul had been unable to say exactly what it was that left him so unsettled. A soft tap at the open door brought him out of his contemplations. "Kelson, my friend. Welcome! What brings the king's blade-master to my humble office so early this glorious morning?"

Kelson took the proffered chair, but was slow to speak.

"Oh my, this must be big!" said Saul, half in jest. "For you to be so *serious*. Is it a problem with my grandson? Is he causing difficulties for you?"

"No *problem* with Marcus, but we need to discuss where he is in his training."

Saul's brow wrinkled in worry and surprise. "He isn't developing the way he should? Is he not applying himself to your satisfaction?"

"You tested the boy for *gift*." He said it more as a fact, not as a question.

"And you know this because?"

"He told me so. I asked him how it went and he said 'not as we thought it would'. So I asked him how he thought it would go. 'Perhaps with a little indication of *gift*'. 'But that wasn't what happened?' I asked him. 'No. That wasn't what happened.' He seemed disappointed."

Clever boy, clever answer thought Saul. Not a lie exactly. Not exactly truth, either. "But there is something that still troubles you, yes?"

Kelson sighed, searching for the right words. "It isn't that he's not developing as he should. Quite the contrary, actually. In the two turnings since I spoke to you last, Marcus has made huge strides in his blade work. He has passed beyond my capacity to teach him further." Again Kelson paused, collecting his thoughts. "You know how the training goes. You went through it yourself when you were young. First there is focus on the fundamentals: footwork, positioning, form .Then we transition to moves and strategy, both defensive and offensive. We discipline out any tendencies to weakness in form, or recurring patterns that would leave our young blades-men vulnerable to an able opponent. It takes time, even turns, to develop a truly capable blades-man."

"But you said Marcus had surpassed..."

"...surpassed my ability to teach. I told you turnings ago that Marcus had developed quickly. But in the time since then, his development has been, well, I don't really know how to describe it. No one, not even the best blades-men in the King's Guard, can touch him. I can't touch him. His 'footwork, positioning and forms' are flawless. Conventional moves are useless against him. And when I try something unorthodox? It might *almost* work, but only that one time, if at all. Normally I would say this is all incredibly good. But here's the thing: he never goes on the offense. He spars purely and exclusively on the defense. So he never wins his matches. Rather, they always end in a protracted draw. When he and I are sparring, I *know* he sees opportunities to strike me down. What's more, he knows that I know, by giving me a wink or a light tap on an unprotected area when I leave myself vulnerable. It's one thing to do it to me, but he does this to all of his opponents. They see it as taunting, so they fall into a rage. Which only makes it easier for Marcus to defeat them. If defeat is the right word for a consensus draw. This seven-day it came to a head. No one is willing to spar with him, to bear the humiliation of another protracted session without hope of prevailing. So, he is left to spar with me. And quite frankly, I don't enjoy it any more than the others. I have mentioned all of this to him. He nods in understanding, then just shrugs and walks away. I am at a loss on what more to do with him. But I have a suggestion for you to consider."

"Kelson, I have never known you to say so much at one sitting. Most of the time I feel fortunate to pull a sentence or two out of you. Obviously, this really has you frustrated. Of course, I can talk to the boy and see if he will open up to me. But it might be useless if you think he is now beyond your ability to teach further. What is your suggestion for him? Remember, he's still only a hand-and two, though he is nearing his birth anniversary."

"Saul, your service to the King, and presumably that will be the boy's future service as well, is in counsel. And if necessary, provide physical protection of the royal family. It is why you, and your fathers before you, have carried the heraldic mage-blade. And it's why you became a blades-man. And it is why I now train Marcus. I know, I know this might sound inconsistent with his future responsibilities, but would you consider turning him over to Bow-master Carston Montague for training in ranged weapons?"

"Ranged weapons? Train him to become an archer? That isn't the kind of conflict a king's-mage is likely to enjoin."

"Yes, I know. But I suggest it be more than 'archer'. I would see him trained in long-bow, cross-bow, and lance- and bo-casting. And in hand-to-hand combat as well. But perhaps somewhat later in melee."

Several moments passed without comment by either man, Kelson knew it best to remain silent as Saul considered his proposal. Saul was not one to rush to a decision. And Kelson knew that a decision would be well-thought and unlikely to be reversed.

Finally, Saul broke the silence. "If what you say is true, and I have no reason to doubt your account, it would be wasteful to continue training with edged weapons. But I would not have him abandon that training completely. Those skills must be frequently practiced. As to the other, I agree. Melee would follow the other, you say? He would not be concurrently trained in both?"

"Ranged weapons, first. He has more growing to do to be capable in the other."

"Hmm. Yes, I believe you are right. And when would you like to have him report to Carston?"

"Perhaps tomorrow? I see no benefit in waiting."

"And what if Carston does not wish to accept him for training? Would we not need to discuss this first, before just turning the boy over?"

Kelson reddened. "Well, I must be honest, Saul. Everyone on the combat training staff knows the situation I've described to you. It has become something of a spectacle to see Marcus spar, depending on his opponent. All of us see future greatness in the lad. Carston himself raised the possibility of training the boy."

"Then it is decided. But one day a seven-day, a full one-day. I would see him continuing to train in edged weapons, agreed?"

"Yes, sir. I will see to it myself." Kelson departed with a respectful bow.

A typical training day for Marcus, six of every seven-day, began early. He arose, attended to his personal needs, and ate a quick breakfast in the combat mess. He would then proceed to the training arena for *tai kai*, the graceful 'forms and position' drill that invariably quieted the mind and gently stretched muscles, making them flexible and less prone to injury. He and the other trainees would then run several laps around the training complex before reporting to a training master.

Marcus stopped before the office of blade-master Kelson, sweating lightly. Second turning would soon be passing into third. But for now, the run had been pleasant. "Sir, Marcus hereby reports for training."

"Yes, Marcus, please come in. I have something for you."

Marcus approached the small desk that seemed to dominate the equally small office that Kelson called his own. On the desk was a box, ornately carved from an exotic dark wood he did not recognize. It was not appropriate for a youth to speak to one's elder (and mentor), unless first spoken to, so he stood there quietly, waiting for Kelson to break the silence.

"Marcus, we have come to an end of your training with me. Although you will be returning on a regular basis to maintain your edged weapon skills, your time here is now complete. You will report to Arch-master Montague this morning and begin training with ranged weapons. I trust you will be as diligent a student with him as you have been with me."

The surprise on Marcus' face would have been hard to miss. "Ranged weapons, sir, as in long- and cross-bows?"

"Yes, and spear and lance and bo-casting as well. And whatever else Carston, uh, Arch-master Montague, might feel useful. But before you go, I have a gift for you." He pointed to the ornate box. "Open it."

Marcus took a step forward to the desk, and placed a finger under the lid. It opened easily. Inside, on a bed of soft-cloth, lay two beautiful short-blades. One was slightly longer than the other. Beside them were two finely tooled sheaths.

"These have been in my family for many turns, even generations. It was always my intention to pass them to my son, as my father passed them to me. But alas, since the plague struck, I

26

have been blessed with neither wife nor son, nor any close family. So I pass them to you, that they might continue their journey forward. They are made of old-steel. I am sure they will serve you well."

Marcus was speechless. Old-steel weapons were rare. They could be honed to an incredible sharpness and would hold their edge when other weapons would not. He reached out and touched them, admiring the intricate engravings on both the handles and the blades. The only other old-steel he knew of was the heraldic mage-blade carried by his grandfather.

"Go ahead. Take them. Hold them. They now belong to you."

Marcus lifted the blades, one in each hand. They fit comfortably and balanced well. He placed the blades into their respective sheaths, closed the lid, and slid the box into the pit of his left arm. "Sir Kelson," bowed Marcus, "I shall treasure these always, not just for their fine workmanship, but for the great respect I have for the giver. May I always bring honor to these blades."

"Well said, young man. Now go, I know a certain bow-master who awaits his newest trainee."

Marcus passed through the armory and walked to the training area dedicated to ranged weapons. One side of the building held metal bars and circular disks, carefully stacked and organized. He puzzled over their function until he saw several men repeatedly lifting and rolling them up to their chests. Several others were lying on low benches, lifting weights from the floor and pushing them up over their heads. He thought for a moment. *It makes sense. It will take a lot more strength to wield a long-bow than a long-blade.* He made his way farther along to the archery range, finding Master Montague carefully examining and testing a long-bow. "Sir

Montague, trainee Marcus reporting." He then stood silently waiting for a reply.

Carston gave Marcus an evaluating eye, head to toe and back again. "You are tall for hand and three, but you will need more meat on your bones to become a good bow-man. Report to the armory and look up Archer Lance. He will get you started on the weights. Come see me in a couple of seven-days." With that, Carston went back to examining the bow.

Sensing a clear dismissal, Marcus turned and retraced his steps to the armory. A few inquiries and he located Archer Lance. He relayed the instructions given him by Arch-master Montague.

Lance gave him the same head-toe-head exam. "Hmm. Yes, you will need greater upper chest and arm strength for the long-bow, but you look strong enough for the cross-bow, and maybe even a casting-lance. Let's get started on weights for now. Follow me."

Marcus spent the remainder of the morning learning how to properly lift weights. By noon his muscles were sore and he was tired.

Lance was a kind man, and saw the distress. "Let's break for lunch. I think an introduction to cross-bow would be a good idea for this after mid-day. More weight training would be of little benefit... at least, until tomorrow," He said with a laugh.

Marcus smiled outwardly but groaned within.

"This is a cross-bow, as you well know. They come in a variety of sizes, the smallest of which you are holding in your hands. I'm probably speaking the obvious, but so be it. The cross-bow shoots bolts, not arrows. Bolts are thicker and shorter than arrows, and have a shorter range. Notwithstanding the differences, aiming and shooting are similar for both. The cross-bow takes as much strength to draw as a long-bow, which means they do not necessarily sacrifice effectiveness in combat. However, due to their length, arrows are more effective at longer ranges and have greater penetrating power. In short, cross-bows rely on impact, arrows on penetration. Are you with me so far?"

Marcus nodded politely, even though none of this was any great revelation to him.

"At the bottom of the cross-bow is the foot-claw or stirrup. When loading the cross-bow, you must carefully and firmly place your foot in the claw. Most injuries are from doing this improperly." Lance paused for effect. "Let me repeat, Marcus, most all injuries with cross-bows are from not following this simple rule."

Again, Marcus nodded politely. This was something new to understand and important to remember.

"The string of a cross-bow is made of many strands of fiber, typically rope-weed. Sometimes we use sinew or rawhide. This string is made of rope-weed. Feel it."

Marcus ran the limp line through his hand and fingers.

"Feels a bit slippery, yes? We put tallow or beeswax on the strings to keep them supple. And to protect them from moisture." There was a brief reflective pause. "Yeah, sometimes even we fight in the rain," he said with a chuckle. "The bow itself is usually made of astor-wood, covered in horn. It is tough. A bigger cross-bow has a longer and thicker bow. Greater power means it's harder to charge. No surprise there. At the back of the bow there is a notch. We use it for rope-loading the bow. More about that later. The last three parts of the bow are the rail, trigger and trigger box. I suppose their use is pretty obvious, right?"

Marcus nodded in agreement.

"Now for the bolts. A bigger cross-bow uses a longer and heavier bolt. Bolts have three vanes. Bolt goes on the rail with one vane up, vertical to the rail. The notch on the bolt must lie horizontal to the rail. Bolts should match the cross-bow for best performance. Now, on to the actual use of the cross-bow. There are three basic ways of loading, or charging, a cross-bow. Which method you use will depend on your strength and power of the bow. Easiest way is by hand. There is also a rope method, and for the largest of the cross-bows, a hand-winch. Let me show you how it's done by hand." Lance placed his foot firmly into the stirrup with an exaggerated display of pressing his foot to the ground. He looked at Marcus, who nodded in understanding. He then grasped the string in both hands and pulled it up the rail until a audible click was heard. "Charged." He then flipped down a small lever next to the trigger box. "And made safe." He picked up a bolt from a quiver hanging on a near-by post, placed it on the cross-bow rail, and allowed it to fall into the trigger box. Looking to make sure the bolt was knocked fully to the string, he turned, flipped the safe switch to the upright position, and cast the bolt at a target some eight paces down range. The bolt struck the center. "Any questions before you try?"

Marcus shook his head and took the cross-bow. He followed the same procedure, charging the cross-bow as he had been shown. He then aimed and cast. The recoil was a bit more than he anticipated. The bolt hit the target, but far from the center.

"Well, not too bad for the first time. I'm SURE you are going to get better with practice. And you will be getting lots and lots of practice! Hah!"

———

Mastering the cross-bow had been difficult for Marcus. He had gotten much stronger through his daily work with weights, but still lacked the strength to manage the large winch-loaded weapons. He had made it to the mid-sized bows, though. It took a full turning to achieve any great accuracy with even the small cross-bow. The break-through came the day, in frustration with an errant bolt. Marcus simply cast *gift* and mentally commanded the bolt back on line. To his utter amazement, the bolt did just that! It turned slightly in flight and embedded itself in the heart of the distant target. He repeated the shot and the application of *gift* again, with the same result. Consecutive heart shots brought immediate attention, attention Marcus did not desire. So he chose other parts of the target, rather than the center.

The next day was his sixth-day training in edged weapons. Marcus has asked previously, a seven-day past, if he might focus on blade casting. It was a somewhat lateral skill with which Marcus had only passing experience. He was far from proficient. Having received permission, he retrieved a handful of casting blades and retired to the throwing gallery. Thankfully, no one else was there and he had a throwing lane to himself. Throwing a blade without spin took considerable practice. The blade was held parallel and against the middle finger and was thrown back-to-front in a horizontal move. Marcus took the first blade and threw it, focusing *gift* to keep it on-target and free from spin. He could see the blade in its flight, fluttering slightly to stabilize then shifting course to embed itself in the target's heart. He repeated this over and over, until it became second nature to do so. Marcus loved blades, especially the two he had been given by Kelson the turning previous. Now, for the first time, he saw them as a viable weapon in his personal armory. He would tell no one of this strange development. Well, except his Grandfather. Problem was, his Grandfather was loathe to discuss *anything* concerning *gift*. Marcus had touched the old man's mind enough to know why. Saul was terrified of the power that he had shown. And he was unwilling to risk unleashing it again with the possibility of doing him harm.

Saul had been detained late in the service of the King. He sent a messenger to advise Marcus of the delay, with instructions to meet him in the castle kitchen for a late dinner together. The days had shortened and their quarters were dark by the time they returned. As they entered, Marcus seized the opportunity to light the candles in the room with a light cast of *gift*.

Saul froze mid-step and stared at Marcus. "You did that! What if..."

"...what if *what*, Grandfather? What if I had been unable to control my *gift* and had destroyed the room again? Is this what you fear so much, why you refuse to even mention *gift* to me in any way? I live with *gift*, every day. We need to talk about it. Now, before I actually do something dangerous."

Saul seemed to wilt before his eyes. "Yes, you are right. And yes, I have been afraid of this day for a very long time. Is there something in particular you want to ask?"

Marcus grunted. "Really? Probably no more than a hand-fist *somethings*. But there is one *something* in particular I want to ask. It's about what happened yesterday, and repeated itself today." Marcus then proceeded to tell his grandfather about changing the direction of both bolts and blades, simply through the casting of *gift*.

Saul listened in stunned silence. Rather than speaking, he plucked a light goose-feather from a pillow on the sofa and tossed it into the air. There it hung, drifting on a small current of air. "Push that to me."

Marcus shrugged, and mentally pushed the feather in his grandfather's direction. The effort was so slight he could barely sense his use of *gift*.

"*Earth-gift*. But you are able to use it without any words of power?"

Marcus shook his head. "No. It's just something I focus on doing. And it happens. It's much like casting flame, but more natural."

Saul sat and invited Marcus to do the same. "The ability is called *gift-casting*. To do so without words of power is exceedingly rare. You haven't shown anyone this ability, have you?"

"No. After I had put a bolt into the target's heart four or five times people started to notice. So I shifted my aim to other parts of the target. When I cast blades after mid-day, I was alone. I have not forgotten your instructions to keep such things between the two of us."

Saul released a sigh of relief "Thank goodness. The *fata* alone know how others would react if they knew of this. What *else* can you do, besides this *gift-casting*.

Marcus thought for a moment. He did not relish telling a lie, especially to his grandfather. But the ability to mind-touch was something he felt he should, at least for the time being, keep to himself. "No, nothing I can share. There are probably some things I'm doing unconsciously. Without more learning about *gift* I don't even realize what I can and can't do, what is normal and what is not."

Saul was quiet a while longer. "There is another reason I have been reluctant to teach you about *gift*. It's because I don't know much about it myself. It's time for a bit of honesty, son. I am the king's Lord High-*mage*, but it is a position I inherited, more than earned. I have *gift*, but it is not overly strong. I am called on frequently to counsel the King, but I do so out of common sense and the wisdom of an old man. There is no... *vigor*... in my advice. I think that is why the King has secured an additional mage to advise him."

Saul got up from his chair and went to bedroom, indicating for Marcus to follow. In the corner of the room was a large chest. Saul took a key from the shelf above, unlocked it, and lifted the lid. He removed several robes, small clothes and outdoor wear, placing them on the floor. When he reached the bottom, he removed a package wrapped tightly in what appeared to be expensive seal-skin. "This," said Saul with a bit of resignation, "is the history of our family. It goes back over four-hand generations. Yes, our position of Lord High-mage to the kings and queens of Iber go back that far. To the very founding of Iber itself. Each Lord High-mage is required to contribute exactly one page to this history. I have written mine, including the account of your birth and your mother's death. This record is yours to continue, once I have passed." Saul took a deep breath. "But you need to study it now. And ask questions if you have them. I trust you will treasure it as an invaluable and irreplaceable part of our history. And that of the Kingdom. In addition, there is much about *gift* to be found within its pages. Each mage who has written, has added his own insights, with the intent that future generations might have a small advantage in their service to Iber's kings and queens. Unfortunately, the earliest chapters, the first hand and five, are written in *Kult*. Yes, our forefathers retained the use of *Kult* for a that many generations. But along the way there was a High-mage who couldn't or didn't pass the language forward. So the last two hand and five chapters are written in *Turga*." He passed the parcel to Marcus. "As I said, there is much to learn here. I give it to you now, to study. Keep it dry, of course. The oldest parchments are over a hand-fist old and have become quite fragile. Perhaps some day you will find a way to translate the earlier *Kult* records. I and some of my predecessors have tried. All with more interest than success."

Marcus reverently took the parcel with a solemn promise to guard it with his life.

"There is one more thing to tell you." Saul unbuckled the long-blade from his waist. "This is the blade of the High Lord-mage of Iber. It is what we call the heraldic mage-blade. Like the manuscript you hold, it has, been a part of our family from the founding of Iber. It is of old-steel, like the daggers gifted you by Carston. It is inlaid with silver. And like the history, it too is for you. But not yet. It is a symbol of my position with the King, and I cannot relinquish it to you until my term of service or my life has come to an end."

The conversation was over. Marcus retired to his room to consider all he had learned this night.

Marcus' bedroom was small and its furnishings were meager: desk, chair, wooden chest (clothes, mostly), a shallow shelf, and a narrow bed. He entered, cast flame to light the candles, and placed the bundled record on the desk. He sat quietly considering his next action. He was burning with curiosity. Should he open the history now? If not now, when? Curiosity prevailed. He carefully untied the bundle and reverently folded back the two layers of seal-skin wrapping. Inside was a wooden box, covered in dull copper. Lifting its lid, Marcus found an eisen-glass, like those used by the weak-eyed to enlarge that which was small and difficult to see. Beneath the eisen-glass lay the written record, a stack of individual, unbound pages. Each page was thick and of highest-quality parchment, together about two-fingers high. Progressive age was reflected in their condition, with the oldest records stiff and much darkened by antiquity. The top sheet, however, was newly composed, clearly, his grandfather's recently-written account. He lay it aside and examined the second sheet, written by his great-grandfather. The need for an eisen-glass was clear. Both were written in a small, tight script, on both sides, as were the subsequent sheets. Clearly, each author had taken his or her instructions seriously, and made much effort to record as much information as possible with the one-page restriction imposed upon them by tradition and ancient command. It would take time, many days, perhaps turns, to work his way through it all. Carefully, he lifted the majority of pages to peek at the oldest. They were much darkened, especially around the edges. And written in *Kult*, a language he recognized by form but not by understanding. Its characters were different than those used by *Turga* and *Rontal*. He mentally resolved to find a way to translate the entirely of it all, somehow, within his lifetime.

Marcus turned back to the first page, his grandfather's record, and began to read.

I, Saul Aurelius, Lord High-mage of Iber, do write this with my own hand, and swear by the fata *themselves it is a true and faithful record of the events in my day. I was born one hand one fists, four-hands and two, from the founding of Iber, on the third turning second seven-day and four. My parents were Victor Aurelius and Maren Melcor, daughter of Lord Karol Melcor and his wife Amelia Dunsworth. The Melcor and Dunsworth were families of long tradition in gift, but alas, short in fortune. I emerged with only a modest level of gift when I reached maturity. After a long courtship, imposed upon us by King Agrippa, I took his daughter, Susanna to wife at the age of three-hands eight.*

Marcus knew this story. King Agrippa felt there were stronger political connections for his daughter than the son of his Lord High-mage. This meant *wealthier families*, his grandfather had explained. But Saul and Susanna had been close friends from childhood. She was determined to have him as her husband. And no one else. It became a test of wills. The King, faced with the embarrassment of a spinster daughter (with diminishing value to potential suitors), finally relented. Susanna and his grandfather were wed after a hand and seven turn courtship By then, however, Susanna had passed her prime child-bearing age.

Being older,, Susanna and I were blessed with but one conception. She brought forth twins, Bekka and Ramone. Both of our children were amply bestowed with gift. But as is always the case of gifted twins. Ramone suffered a wasting disease following his emergence. He passed away at the age of a hand and four. My Susanna, never of great health, passed at the age of four hands and nine.

Thus ended the first paragraph of his account, occupying a scant three finger-width of written space. The print was small. By candle-light it was difficult to read. Marcus put the parchment away and retired for the night.

The next day was a seventh, a day of rest. After breakfast, Marcus continued with the record of his grandfather. There was much written about the commercial and political affairs of the Kingdom. It was clear that Saul had a high regard for King Justin, and the counsel he had provided over the turns seemed wise. The many entries Saul had made had been recorded in the sequence they had occurred, the majority made before his birth. Marcus finally found further references to his family.

Bekka was highly favored by gift *and was my intended successor. She married High-mage Myron of Sage, he of a wealthy family and himself strong in* earth-gift. *Gift notwithstanding, Lord Myron was struck down by the hand of disease, even while Bekka carried their first-born. She, too, was weakened by the disease that swept the Kingdom. (My father, Victor, wrote much of this malady, believing it had been brought to our land by a mage visiting from the mainland.) Bekka brought forth a son during the height of a sun-darkening, that rarest of events when the moon passes before the sun. If, as some believe, the relative position of the sun and moon influence the power of inherited* gift, *and the attraction of the sun and moon together create the strongest of such events, it might be that the son will be strongly and uniquely* gifted. *The son was a fifth-born, it being the fifth generation from Marcus the Eighth. As dictated by the first King of Iber, and in remembrance of his esteemed Lord High-age, Marcus, each fifth-born high-mage thereafter was to bear his name. Therefore, I named the child Marcus the Ninth, dark-born and heir to the office of Lord High-mage to the King of Iber. Bekka succumbed the night of her son's birth to the rigors of labor and the aforementioned disease. The upbringing and training of her son fell to me in its entirely. I have endeavored to prepare him properly for his future service as my successor, believing that he will be of great value to the present and future kings of Iber.*

At last, Marcus approached the end of his grandfather's record. Saul had spoken very little of Marcus' parents, so much of this was new to him. He knew nothing of the origin of his name, nor the reference to being dark-born. The sheet ended with a lengthy paragraph regarding the new mage, Sinifir, who had attached himself to the king.

"*He maintains a shadowed mind, and therefore a shadowed*

intent. My gift-sense *tells me he is a hard man. Indeed, his counsel to the king reflects a harshness I would never recommend. King Justin listens, and by small degrees has adopted higher taxes with severe penalties for those who do not pay, or pay less that that assessed by the growing number of tax collectors. Making it worse, the King has been persuaded to place tax collection under the direction of this new mage. Thus, turning by turning, Sinifir has gained control over the Kings treasury. Such action is foreign to the King I have served for these many turns, and I have brought it to his attention. As expected, I am treated with great hostility by Sinifir. And the King seems to favor his counsel over mine. I am led to believe Sinifir is a mind-mage, and worse, a dark mage as well. Mind-mages are rare and dark mages rarer still, even creatures of myth, as some believe. But these chronicles affirm their existence. Dark mages have but two pursuits: power and wealth. They avoid exposure, working always behind the seats of power. They glory in the misery and suffering of others. And willingly foment war to fulfill their vile desires. The blood of armies and the lives of men mean little to them, and serve only as the coin of their ambition. Of additional concern is the growing attachment of Sinifir to the King's grandson and potential future heir, Prince Stephan. Each time I see them huddled, which occurs more and more frequently, I wonder why a grown man would spend so much time with a hand-and-eight-turn young man. I fear this bodes poorly for King Justin, his son and anointed heir Crown Prince Jared, and for Iber itself.*

Deciphering the tight script of his grandfather had been difficult and tiring, and the last writings had been depressing, at best. It was growing late in the day and sunlight was waning. And tomorrow would begin another seven-day of intense training. Marcus sealed up the record in its box and double wrapping of seal-skin,, placed the bundle at the bottom of his chest of clothes, and went to have supper with his grandfather.

CHAPTER

FOUR

M arcus had few friends, partly by circumstance but mostly by design. There were few children his age in or near the castle, and his studies left him little time for their associations and the friendship. At a hand's age he had begun training with blades. And after the early emergence of *gift*, Saul counseled him to remain aloof. This changed when Marcus turned hand and four and began his hand- and-fifth turn. He had felt the changes in his body. He had rapidly grown taller and more muscular, with wider shoulders and stronger arms and hands. His voice grew deeper and the fuzz on his cheeks provided much good-natured amusement to the men with whom he trained. He continued to work with ranged weapons and once each seven-day with edged. He finally managed the large winch-loaded cross-bows without difficulty. The distance and accuracy of his arrows and bolts were equal to the better archer. Unless he chose to employ *gift*. In which case he could best them all. He had spent a full turning with spears and lances. These required arm and shoulder strength to cast effectively. Marcus had found that he could trickle small amounts of *gift* into the effort to enhance both his efforts. But he displayed this aspect of his ability with discretion, lest it be noticed.

Marcus had also spent two full turnings with siege weapons: small and large: catapults, ballista and trebuchets. But there wasn't much to learn with them. They were brutes, the blunt tools of ranged weapons. Load a rock (catapults and trebuchets) or a large bolt (ballista), aim, release. Pick up the rubble left behind. When the men in the siege company weren't training, they turned their attention to cards and drink, neither of which had appeal to Marcus. So he looked for other things to do, finding three aspects of siege training that were interesting and potentially useful.

First, there was bo training. A bo was a large wooden staff to which a leather strap was attached, half its length. At the end of the strap was a pouch in which a rather large casting stone could be placed. The stone was thrown in the same manner as a catapult. With practice it was a devastating weapon, capable of disabling or killing a horseman and the beast that carried him. And the bo was equally effective in hand-to-hand melee. The rule, however, was that each bo-bearer had to harvest his own staff, harden it properly over a bed of coals, and attached a strap of his own making. The strap was carefully fitted into a groove that ran the length of the staff, thus not interfering with the bo's action in hand-to-hand combat. Marcus spent four seven-days preparing his own. Everyone agreed, it was of fine workmanship. With practice, and more than a little help from *gift*, Marcus became one of the best bo-casters in the company.

Second, siege weapons were large and required beasts – horses and oxen – to move from place to place. Marcus had never had much experience with draft animals, as this was the usual demesne of the cavalry. So he volunteered to work with the herd-master in tending the animals. Mostly it was a monotonous routine of feeding, currying and combing, and the out-mucking of stalls. The herd-master welcomed Marcus' help, and returned his appreciation by teaching him in the nuances of tack, riding, and harnessing.

Riding a horse was painful at first, but with practice it became tolerable. A Calvary-man he would never be, but at least he could stay on a horse without fear of falling off. Of equal importance, he had learned how to care for the beasts properly.

Marcus discovered that with mind-touch he could sense the general mood of individual animals, as well as the combined herd. On one particular day, one of the large oxen refused to be harnessed. And with an animal of its size, when it didn't want to be placed into service there was little the herd-master could do about it. Marcus used mind-touch and found the ox in pain. He sank health-*gift* into the animal and traced its source to an infected tick bite, at a place where harness straps merged. He brought this to the attention of the herd-master, who waved him off in disregard. But with Marcus' persistence, he did finally examine the ox and was amazed to find the soreness, exactly as it had been described.

"How did you know about this? It's covered with hair."

"Well," Marcus pointed to the ox, "he told me all about it. I looked, and it was right where he said it was."

The herd-master looked at Marcus as if to say *really?* Then realizing that such a thing simply couldn't be, he broke out in laughter. "You had me there, boy. For a moment I thought you were serious! I'll get this taken care of right away. Now tell me. How did you really know about the infection."

Marcus struggled for a plausible explanation. "Well, uh, I saw him favoring that shoulder, so I thought something might be bothering him. It was easy to find once I knew generally where to look." To Marcus' relief, that seemed to satisfy the herd-master.

Marcus continued to experiment with mind-touching the horses and oxen. Horses, he found, tended to be a bit more intelligent, if that were the way to describe them. And among the horses, some were more so than others. It wasn't like he could actually communicate with them, but he could perceive basic emotions and feelings. And he could sooth them with 'peaceful' thoughts. The oxen were consistently *dull*.

The third activity of interest was the mess – cooking for the soldiers. The company cook was a jovial, heavy-set man. 'Yeah, I like me cookin' a wee bit too much,' when Marcus made note of his size. He had several assistants helping with serving and cleaning up. Marcus joined in with them, much to the teasing of his fellow soldiers. Marcus just shrugged with the comment 'just keeping busy'. After a few days Marcus asked if he could observe the cooking and learn how to make *some of those delicious meals* the cook was so proud to prepare and serve. It was not a total exaggeration. The cook knew his trade and took pride in it.

"It's mostly just two things, cookin' and spicen'. There be a handful of good plants, growin' all around us, what makes food taste better." He pulled a small notebook from his apron pocket wherein he had made various plant drawings and notations on their use. "You be wise to copy some of this down, if'n yah be planning on cooking on the hoof. I 'ave a bit of parchment and ink if'n yuh have a mind to."

Marcus took him up on the offer. It took several seven-day evenings, working around the commitment he had with the herdmaster. The cook looked over his shoulder from time to time as he wrote, adding comments and instructions he thought might be useful. In the end Marcus was pleased with his effort, a veritable *cooking-book*.

As Marcus took on a more manly form, the men -- archers, spearmen, blades-men and siege-men -- began treating him more as an equal than a young trainee. With little left to learn, Lance, Carston and Kelson asked him if he would be willing to teach blades. "We still want you to learn melee, but we thought another bit of growing would be appropriate before that. Let's see where you are in, say, half a turn. In the meantime, we're short instructors, especially for the younger ones commencing their training."

"Really? You are short of instructors? I thought your blade- and arch-masters enjoyed teaching."

Lance replied. "Well, they do. But the King has more and more use for them these days. Most have been called up to the regular military."

Marcus gave them a puzzled look. Iber had never maintained a significant standing military. "Why, is Iber worried about an invasion? We are an island. Who would ever try crossing the Betting Sea with an army, and what would they plan on gaining if they did so? It's not like Iber has any cities of gold."

Lance shrugged. "Maybe that's the problem. The King wants someone else's gold."

The blood in Marcus' veins ran chill. *Dark mage. Power and wealth. And war to achieve it.* He would bring this to the attention of his grandfather, though he was sure he was already well aware of such. But yes, he would be happy to teach.

Marcus was amazed to see how much he towered over his cadre of students. They were ten-and-one, some ten-and-two. Though he was but four turns their senior, yet they saw him as a grown man and gave him the appropriate attention and respect.

"Welcome to training in edged weapons. This includes the long-blade, short-blade and casting blades. The most important of these is the long-blade, as it is always your preferred weapon in combat. If you find yourself engaging an opponent with a short-blade, your likelihood of escaping without injury, or worse, is small. Let me repeat, close quarters fighting is unpredictable. The best with small-blades are melee fighters, not blades-men. For the next two turnings you will be focusing on four things: footwork, position, form and focus. Which is the most important aspect of these, in developing effective blades-skill?"

No one was quick to answer. Finally, one boy raised his hand. "Focus, sir?"

"No. Well, yes." Marcus chuckled. "I suppose if you totally

forget what you are doing, you won't survive for long. But I was looking for a different answer. Anyone else?"

A young girl, the only one in the group, raised her hand.

She looked familiar. "Your name?"

"Katrina, sir. It has to be 'position', right?"

"Actually, that's not right, either. The correct answer is *footwork*. The movement of your feet will determine the position and form that follows. Let me illustrate."

And so the classes began. By day he taught, by night and seventh-day he carefully copied page after page of the chronicles onto new sheets of heavy parchment. The copy would be his to annotate with insights and references as they occurred to him. The earliest pages were particularly slow to copy. Knowing nothing of *Kurt*, he could only make painstakingly precise copies of the strange text, character-by-character.

Marcus developed a growing relationship with his trainees, really the first ever friendships with youth of his own approximate age. After a full turning, he was pleased with their progress. He remembered Kelson's early emphasis on fundamentals. *Practice makes permanent. Only perfect practice produces perfect performance.* He drilled this maxim into his students through countless, precise repetitions of footwork, followed by basic positions and forms. His prize student, the one that developed fastest, was Katrina. She practiced with a passion and attention to detail unmatched by the others. It had finally come to him that she was the King's grand-daughter, sister to Prince Stephan, making her his own second cousin. She had changed, grown and matured, since he had seen her last. She was tall and a bit ...

curvy ... for her age. She *seemed* unaware of their family relationship, and Marcus felt no need to disclose it. His grandfather's marriage to Susanna, the King's sister, had not been a popular one with the family. Saul was constantly in the King's presence as his Lord High-mage. This did not make them socially close in any family way, even though by marriage he was the king's uncle.

Marcus had asked how she, a royal, had been selected for blades-training. She had explained. "We who are royals do not pass into the ordinary ranks. We remain forever royals. And we can choose our under-training. So I chose blades. Much to my father's dismay."

Marcus waited for her to go on.

"I know. You are wondering why, right?"

Marcus nodded, still saying nothing.

Katrina bit her lip, obviously hesitant to say more. "I'm fascinated with blades, and..." Finally she blurted out. "Because I do not trust my brother Prince Stephen! *Oh, please don't tell anyone I told you that!*"

Marcus raised his hands. "Your reasons are safe with me. You are not the only one who has voiced concerns. He spends much time with Sinifir, right?"

"You know Sinifir?"

"Know him? No. Know of him? Yes. Perhaps you have a reason to be afraid."

Katrina seemed relieved to have a confidant. A far-away look came into her eyes. "If only you knew. I see what Sinifir has done to Stephen, and to my grandfather, the King. It is not good. And there is no one I can talk to about it. You are my second cousin, right? I can trust you?"

Before he could answer, their conversation was interrupted by blade-master Kelson. "Ah, there you are, Marcus. A word if you would."

Marcus nodded to Katrina, who gave him a sad smile in return and took her leave. He would have much to discuss tonight with his grandfather. Marcus turned his attention to Master Kelson. "Yes?"

"Change of assignment for you. Melee training. Of a sorts. The King has asked that we assemble a few of our best blades-men for full turning, perhaps longer, for special training. You have been particularly requested."

"Requested? By whom? I'm still a trainee myself."

"And yet, one of our best blade-men. Please, Marcus, I didn't make the list. It will take a few days to assemble the rest of those who have been named. Some are from the military or palace guard, some are not. Someone has gone to a lot of trouble to put these names together. So you know, the classes start a seven-day after the next first. We will have to find someone to teach your students during your absence." There was a pause, and a sigh of worry. "Your grandfather and I had always planned for you to take melee training, but not this way. It's *off* in someway. Nothing I've ever seen before. But, *as the King commands*, we are obliged to follow."

Marcus doubted it was the King's idea. This felt like more maneuvering by Sinifir, but the purpose of it escaped him. "As you say, *as the King commands*."

Marcus and his grandfather discussed the special melee training over dinner. Saul had heard of special training planned for select elements of the palace guard, and its cost. But the details Marcus provided were news to him. "What use would the King have for a cadre of melee and blades?" They tossed the question back and forth but came to no clear conclusion. Tomorrow was a sixth day. There would be training, followed by a seventh day, then another seven-day before the special training was scheduled to commence.

As class ended the next day and the students departed, Katrina pressed a small slip of paper into his hand as she walked by. She had obviously lingered, assuring to be the last to leave. Marcus unfolded it and read: *We must visit, but not where we will be seen or heard. Sundown, west palm garden. Please. Come alone. You must not let anyone know. Destroy this.*

The west palm garden was a small area, hard fast to the castle's high west wall. It contained a small artesian spring flowing with brackish water. Bushes and flowering plants did not thrive in the spring's flow, but palm trees seemed to flourish. They grew densely, providing privacy of both sight and sound. Being on the west, the garden fell early into evening darkness. Marcus found Katrina standing in the shadows, waiting.

"*Fata* be blessed, you came!" whispered Katrina as Marcus approached. "Did anyone see you come this way?"

Marcus shook his head. "I was careful, came through the kitchens and west arbors. I would have seen anyone attempting to follow."

Katrina visibly relaxed. "This is about Sinifir, my brother Prince Stephen, and the planned training."

"You know about the melee and blade training?"

"The wall between my bedroom and Stephen's is thin. I hear much more than they realize. Especially if I stand in a certain place next to our adjoining comfort rooms." She gave a smirk. "And pressing a water glass against the wall helps a little as well."

Marcus smiled at the thought. "So what have you heard?"

"Assassins. They are recruiting a team of assassins. Men, and maybe a few women as well, who can carry out their designs for overthrowing the king and seizing the Kingdom. It is all very dark, very evil. They are making short- and long-term plans, the latter for when Stephen completes the next two turns and reaches two hands, and can legally assume the throne. And that is not all."

"There's more?"

"Oh yes! Sinifir is preparing for war."

No surprise there, thought Marcus.

"Caldonia. They are building an army, and plan a small navy as well, to invade the Kingdom of Caldonia. Plunder and return.

They calculate little response from Caldonia or the other mainland kingdoms, given the difficulty in crossing the Betting Sea in pursuit."

"And they discuss this openly?"

"Openly? Hardly. They consider Stephen's room completely secure, with its stone walls and location near the end of the family residence hall. Hah! If they only knew."

"And fortunately, they do not. If they did, your life..."

"... wouldn't be worth a straw in a raging flame. I know. That's why I can't tell anyone. I don't know whom to trust, except you, cousin. And what am I, are we, to do about this? Sinifir has the King's total confidence. As for the army, Sinifir has convinced him there is a growing Caldonian threat and Iber must prepare for its defense. It's all crazy, we know, but such is the control Sinifir holds." She paused. "I have told you what I know, and if I am gone much longer I shall certainly be missed." She turned and walked swiftly away, leaving Marcus alone in the shadows. He would wait a while longer lest their departures be seen to coincide.

At length, Marcus returned to his room using a different route than the one used by Katrina. His grandfather was away, not particularly unusual as this happened frequently. He fell onto his bed, thinking through all he had learned that evening. *Assassins!* The very word implied evil in its darkest form. And *war?* Who would believe that? Iber had not seen war, civil or foreign, for over a hand fist of turns. No one had time, nor strength in numbers, for such. Survival on this remote, foreboding island was enough of a fight all by itself. *Invade Caldonia?* Iber's army wouldn't stand a chance. Caldonia would most certainly return the fight, Betting Sea notwithstanding. Actually, it wouldn't matter if they did or not. If not overthrown by Caldonia, there would be an internal revolt against King Justin and the royal line would come pass to...?. Who would be left to rule? It wouldn't matter. Mind-mage Sinifir would survive and become the power behind any throne that arose.

The next day was a seventh and there were no classes to teach.

Saul had obviously been out late, as he was slow to arise. Marcus finished first-meal and waited patiently. When his grandfather finally came to the table, it was clear he was in a peckish mood. "Damn silliness, all this military spending. These are things we cannot afford. But no matter how much I argue the point, there is Sinifir whispering in the King's ear."

"Perhaps I can shed some light on the matter," said Marcus in a low voice, nearly in a whisper.

"What? You know something I don't? Well, out with it!"

So Marcus replayed all the events of the last several days. When he finished, Saul sat in stunned silence. "*Fata* help us.! Sinifir truly is a dark mage, as I suspected."

"Yes, so it would appear. But grandfather, knowing it is one thing, doing something about it quite another. Sometimes the greatest and most obvious threats are the hardest to recognize, appreciate overcome. It happens when people with power control those who have none. And right now you and the royals appear to be powerless against the wiles of Sinifir."

"Yes, it is as you say. But we might have a way of thwarting these plans of Sinifir and Stephen, at least for a while. Leave it to me for the time being."

CHAPTER
FIVE

Marcus had copied his way through all three-hands and six pages of family history written in *Turga*. And he had copied a few of the first hand and five written in *Kurt*. The latter was slow, character by character. All together the history spanned four-hand-and-one generations. Several of those who had written had been lateral to the main family line. But the office of Lord High-mage had always returned, eventually, to the direct family line from Marcus Aurelius the First. Although *Kult* had been lost as a common language two-hands and five generations earlier, remnants, scattered words of power, clearly remained. Else access to *gift* would have been lost as well. It seemed clear to Marcus that interest in *Kult* (and therefore how to speak it properly) had waned over the turns here in the isolated Kingdom of Iber. With its decline, access to additional powers of *gift* had likewise been lost. A few, like those mentioned by his grandfather, had made an effort to revive its understanding and use. But overall it had been a feeble effort at best. From this, Marcus had come to the conclusion that *gift* itself had come to hold less and less interest to the royals and high families. In a way, he reflected, this was understandable. *Gift* had weakened among the common people. For those in possession, it was considered as much a nuisance as asset. With less attention to hereditary lines, it had weakened. It was ignored when detected. And too often left undeveloped when found. And those with *gift*, or even an interest in it, were ridiculed at best, feared at worst. It was like faith in the *fata*, dying a slow but inevitable death. Well, except for those like Sinifir, his grandfather, and a few royals. These knew all too well the utility of *gift*. For ill or good, *gift* held real power.

Marcus had no way of understanding the *kurt* words he copied. Words like *fo* (flame) and *lu* (light) he had heard before and knew. But he did not know the characters that represented them. Not knowing where else to turn, or to whom he *might* turn, he decided to visit the widely disparaged *Kentuck the Crazy*. But first, Marcus had to find him. He left after the first-meal discussion with his grandfather and headed in the direction of the Chapel of Alexa. Seventh-day was the 'busy day' for the faithful. Inside. He found two old priest-mages and four visitors. He approached the older-looking of the two and waited until the priest-mage acknowledge his presence.

A spark of hope arose in the man's eyes. "Hello, young man. Have you come to give alms?" With a sigh he continued, "Or simply worship the power and benevolence of the *fata*."

The sixth virtue of the *fata* suddenly came to his mind. *Be generous to the poor and to those who serve the* fata. "Alms, of course," said Marcus, retrieving his belt-purse and placing a full silver into the mage's hand. A silver, being the equivalent of two-hand coppers, was a considerable gift.

"Oh! May the *fata* bless you!"

"Yes, indeed! But I would also like some information."

The mage looked warily at Marcus. "You are not bribing me, are you young man?"

"No, sir. The alms-giving is sincere. But perhaps you can help me find a friend of a friend. I am afraid he is held in low regard, even though a mage he is. Or once was."

"Ah, in that case I will do what I can. And this 'friend-of-a-friend'? His name?"

Marcus braced himself for the ridicule he expected to receive. "His name is *Kentuck*. Some refer to him as *Kentuck the Crazy*. I would speak to him of things in my family's distant past."

Rather than the expected reply, the old mage gave Marcus a sad look and mournful sigh. "Kentuck. He was once a good mage. And a good friend. But I think he got lost along the way, spending way too much time in archives with musty old manuscripts. Some say the dust affected his mind. Others say his imagination got away from him. In any case, the gentle man I knew is long gone, leaving, as you say, a crazy man in his stead."

"He lives? And you know where I can find him?"

"Oh yes, he lives, but very much alone. And not far from here. His life is one of scavenging for food, sometimes begging. And in desperate times he has been known to help himself without invitation to the food of others. And he likes his drink when he can get it." The mage hesitated and began speaking with careful words. "He is harmless. He is tolerated. And he is avoided. He is unwashed, unclean if you know what I mean. His body odor is highly offensive. Always, as he no longer bathes himself nor launders his clothes."

"I get the picture, yes. You say he lives nearby?"

"You are determined then, to see him? "

Marcus nodded.

"Very well. Go two streets farther, and you will see a hovel on the right, well above the way. There is considerable garbage about the place. Unpleasant as he is, we check in on him from time to time, especially if we don't see him around. Be advised, though, he is no longer swift of foot. So after you knock, give him time to answer." The mage went suddenly tense and a far-away look came to his eyes. His voice changed. *"The Fata speak. You have a great* work to do. To right an ancient wrong. *By the power of four you will protect, persuade and prevail over the kingdoms who wronged your people in the distant past."* The priest-mage shook his head. Oh, now, where were we? Yes, you were just leaving. You might take him some food. He is always in want of a meal."

"Thank you. I shall."

The directions, though meager, were sufficient. Marcus made his way carefully around piles of detritus and rapped sharply on the hovel door. And waited. He knocked again. And waited. There was finally a rustle of movement and the door swung open. As the old mage had predicted, the smell was overwhelming.

"What you want? Can't you see I'm busy? Hah! Busy? As if Kentuck the Crazy has anything someone else would want or need. Did you bring me any food?"

Marcus pulled a loaf of bread from the outside pocket of his cape, glad that he had followed the advice of the priest-mage.

Kentuck's eyes opened wide "Food? You brought me *food? Fata* be blessed! Old Kentuck has not eaten much for a full two-day. Come in. Oh, please come in. And give me the bread!" He literally snatched the loaf from Marcus' grasp.

Marcus braced himself against the smells and entered.

Kentuck tore pieces of bread and stuck them in his mouth, drinking from a dingy flagon of water between bites. Only when the loaf was half gone and Kentuck had apparently had his fill, did he turn to Marcus. "What business do you have for Crazy Kentuck? It must be important, to come into this stink-hole I call home. Don't look surprised, I know how bad it is. It's just that I don't care anymore. No one cares for Crazy Kentuck, so he doesn't care about them." Then sadly, "nor about himself. There you have it. My life wrapped in the shell of a nut. Now there is only waiting for the end. It all ends with me, everything I know. It ends with me. Now tell me, who are you and what do you want with Crazy Kentuck?"

"My name is Marcus, Marcus Aurelius. I am..."

Kentuck interrupted sharply. "Say no more. I know exactly who you are. Son of Bekka and Lord Myron of Sage. Grandson of Saul the Skeptic. And Marcus Aurelius you say? You are a fifth in the generations of Marcus? Now, *that* is indeed interesting. Hmm. Most interesting indeed."

"You knew my parents and my grandfather. And my family history?"

"Knew, know. Yes. Spoke to your parents a few times. Know your grandfather well. At least I did, many turns ago, when your mother was but a child. Before the passion of learning *Kult* overtook me."

"*Kult?* That is why I have come to see you. I have a family record..."

Again he was interrupted by Kentuck. "Yes, the Chronicles of the Lord High-mages of Iber. I've seen it. Saul even let me *touch* it turns ago. I begged him to let me study it, translate it if I could. But he adamantly refused. It 'wasn't for me to read'. Arrogant piece of ... Forgive me. He's your grandfather and I'm sure you love him. He's done his duty to you ever since your parents passed." There was a pause. "So you have it now, you say? And you want old Kentuck's help translating it? Well, it's too late. Kentuck's eyes are not what they used to be. Can't see much of anything anymore. Certainly not a dusty manuscript written in such small script it takes an eisen-glass to see it, let alone read."

Marcus looked into the clouded eyes of Kentuck. "I understand, sir, when you say it ends with you, all you know ends with you. But... it doesn't have to, not really. Not if you pass everything you know on to me." Marcus could feel his passion rise. "I want, no, I *must* read the chronicle, in its entirely. Including the older pages in *Kult*. Too much has already been lost. I fear if I do it not, it could all be lost forever. And not just the history of Iber, but so much about *gift*. And *that* we cannot allow, for the safety of our kingdom and the world. And I believe you are the only one here in Iber able to teach me."

"You want to learn *Kult*? You want me to teach you *Kult*?"

Marcus nodded and meekly replied "Yes, sir. That's what I want."

Kentuck laughed uproariously. "You want *me* to teach *you* what has taken *me* a lifetime to learn by myself? Sorry, boy, cannot, will not happen." The laugh morphed into a great cough. There was a touch of blood at the corner of his mouth. In a serious voice he continued. "Old Kentuck has but a short time left in this life. I feel it in my bones. Even now, I'm too weak even to go beg for food." He sighed in regret. "Oh, boy, that you had come to me earlier. Even just a few turns ago. But *tiemp* cannot be denied. I might be manipulated perhaps a little. But not denied. In the end it takes us all."

"*Tiemp?*"

"*Tiemp*. Time. Time, my boy, time. It's said the old ones could move themselves around in it a bit. But as I said, in the end it takes us all. So I cannot teach you *Kult*, no *tiemp* remaining." A moment later he resumed, thoughtfully. "But perhaps I can help you teach yourself."

Marcus gave him a puzzled look. "Teach myself?"

Kentuck, frustrated: "You can *read* can't you?" Kentuck, apologetically, continued. "Of course you can." He rose slowly on stiff legs and shuffled to a weathered wooden chest in the corner of the small room. He lifted its lid, rummaged through the contents, and came out with a wrapped bundle. It was not that much different in size and shape than the box containing the Chronicle. "I had once tried to give this to the Chapel of Alexa, but they said it stank and refused to accept it. In my hubris, my spite, I decided to let it die with me. But you give me hope, Marcus. You give me a ray of actual hope." He handed the boy the bundle. "On these pages is the entirely of the *Kult-Turga* cross reference I have worked on for the latter half of my life. It has been tedious, at best. But towards the last my understanding increased. I found it possible to make it grow somewhat faster. My biggest problem has always been finding source material. I've gone through the chapel's library, gleaned what I could, and looked everywhere I could imagine. What I found were mostly old ballads, rich in words but poor in content. T'was why I wanted to work on your mage chronicle. That would have helped immensely. But no, your grandfather did not believe me. He thought my work was foolishness. He said it was impossible to resurrect *Kult*. It's why I called him Saul the Skeptic. Oh, would that we lived on the mainland! I'm sure there are many, many old documents hidden away that would have helped me. You know, I have even found a few examples of *Elken* in my research? Now *that* would be something, for all of us who desire to unlock the true power of *gift*." His cough returned, worse than before. Again, there was fresh blood on his lips. His voice was softer, more labored: "Take it, Marcus, and continue my work. Otherwise, it will surely die with me." He rose slowly, painfully, and pointed to the door. "Go, and may the *fata* bless you for giving this old man some peace at the end of his troubled life. And some bread."

Marcus took the bundle of manuscripts and left, determined to return with more food in the following days. It was not to be. When he returned of evening a two days hence, it was only to find that *Kentuck the Crazy* had passed. He had been found by his few friends, dead, with a contented smile upon his lips.

CHAPTER

SIX

The seven-day preceding melee training had passed much too quickly. The first day of melee found Marcus in a large assembly hall in the northwest corner of the training complex. It was a room foreign to him. There were about three-hand men present, along with a few tough-looking women. The posture, attitude and dress of the majority were clear indications they were not drawn from the military or wealthy. Marcus looked at them with curiosity. They returned his gaze with a sneering disgust. The thought *it wouldn't take much to turn these into assassins* passed quickly through his mind.

With a resigned voice, an officer of the King's Guard (lieutenant? captain? major? hard to tell from a distance) drew everyone's attention and called the assembly to order. "Thank you for coming. My first task will be to get you organized into some kind of order according to your individual skill levels."

He was rudely interrupted by an uncultured voice yelling. "Wrong. First order uh business is when we be getting' paid." Another yelled. "And how much it be!" Guffaws from the hoard of raucous recruits quickly followed.

The captain (Marcus could now see the chevrons on his sleeve, *Captain of the King's Guard*) calmly waited until the tumult died down. "All in good time. You will be paid each seven-day, upon satisfactory completion of that seven-day's training."

"Well, I wannit now, or I'm outta here" shouted the same heckler as before.

The captain shrugged. "Your choice. No one is forcing you to stay." About one-in-four of those present turned and walked out the door. "I guess that settled that," he said, with some relief in his voice. "Now, I need you to form two lines, one on my left and one on my right. On my left I want those who have received formal training in blades. Those on my right without formal training, experience notwithstanding. I then want your two lines to turn and face each other."

It took a few moments to get formed up. Interestingly, the two lines were reasonably equal in length. Marcus was young and growing, but was already tall for a man, about nine hands last time he had been measured. The man across from him was much larger, at least a full hand taller and easily half again his weight. He had small, hard eyes and a scar that stretched from his left ear to the bottom of his chin. The cut had been poorly treated, and therefore, had poorly healed. He had large, knurled hands, reflecting a life accustomed to hard manual labor. *And more than likely, a generous share of brawls and bar fights. Perfect for melee, probably not subtle enough for an assassin.*

Seeing everyone lined up, the captain instructed each pair to go to the back of the gallery where a table was stacked with wooden long-blades.

"When you have armed yourselves, I want you to come forward, two pairs at a time, and engage in blade-to-blade combat. Winners to my right, losers to my left. You win when your opponent concedes or can no longer fight. First two pairs, to the front."

Marcus estimated about a hand-and-five pairs within the room.

His partner (opponent?) was anxious to fight and tried to pull him to the front. Marcus was reluctant to do so, much to the big man's annoyance. They finally settled about half-way back.

Marcus was curious to see if formal training provided much advantage. Apparently it did, as the first two 'untrained' combatants quickly fell to the superior footwork and form of their trained opponents. The second group ended in the opposite. Both untrained opponents were agile, their quickness provided for lengthy exchanges of thrust and parry, and ultimate success. By the time it was Marcus' turn, four groups of four had competed. Trained blades-men held the edge, a hand to six. Three trained and two untrained blades-men had impressed him. The other hand-and-one were fair to mediocre at best.

"Your name?" asked Marcus, politely.

His opponent grunted. "You don't be needin' it. You gonna be outta here so fast there be no point in learnin' it."

Marcus nodded and took a defensive stance. The captain shouted "GO" and the action began.

For a big man, his opponent was quite fast. He rushed Marcus, thinking to catch him off guard. But Marcus had used mind-touch and knew his opponents intent. He stepped aside, stuck out a foot, and sent the man sprawling. It could have ended there with a quick move and thrust to the throat. But no, Marcus wanted to see more of his opponent. The large man picked himself up from the floor, dusted himself off, and faced Marcus again.

"Dirty fighter. Trip a man rather than fight'em face-to-face. I'll show you what a real blade fight is all about." Again the man rushed at Marcus, who calmly stepped to the side, parried the blow, and brought the broad side of the long-blade down sharply across the knuckles of his opponent's right hand. He howled in pain.

"You're down a hand. Do you want to continue?" asked Marcus. The big man growled something unintelligible, more animal than human. "Yeah, one more time, you greppin' peacock." This time, the exchange took longer. But not a lot longer. The big man took four or five futile swipes at Marcus, moves that were predictable even without the assist of mind-touch. After one last spectacular miss, Marcus stepped in, blocked his opponent's arm, and delivered a heavy blow to the man's chest. He let the wooden blade slip through his hand rather than piercing him to the heart. Big man reacted in shock, looking down at the blade point still held against his chest.

Marcus: "You lose."

Big man. "I lose." Saying nothing else, he went to join the other defeated opponents to the captain's left.

Winners fought winners, losers fought losers. Several matches were close. Marcus' were not. He finally faced the only other remaining undefeated blades-man. He was one of the non-trained men that had earlier caught his eye. The boy-man was older than Marcus, somewhere between late teens and two-hand four. It was hard to tell. He had dark, intelligent eyes and was about Marcus' height. And he had a hungry leanness that shouted *lethal*. This was the winners' match, and everyone crowded in to see the two erstwhile champions go head-to-head.

Marcus reached and lightly touched his opponent's mind. His intended move was clear, but it was a move too simple for such a clever blades-man. There was deception afoot, he was sure. When the boy-man moved forward in his first move, Marcus feinted to defend, but then stepped back rather than engaging. And as Marcus had suspected, the young man flipped the blade to his other hand and swiped through from an entirely different direction. It was a much-practiced move, so sudden and so unexpected that Marcus would surely have been struck down had he not retreated. They stood a pace apart, appraising each other, surprise in one set of eyes, wariness in the other.

"I thought I had you there. Don't miss very often."

Marcus realized he had to end this quickly. His natural style was to be on the defense. But he was not confident he would prevail against this fellow, even with the advantage of mind-touch.

So he feinted left, right, left, finally getting within the boy-man's guard. Through mind-touch, his defensive moves were clear and followed to plan. Marcus blocked a final move and sliced his wooden long-blade up through the boy's exposed groin. He fell like a sack of sand, knowing that if it had been a real blade, he would be holding his entrails in his hands.

The crowd was silent. Neither of them was a crowd favorite, but trained vs. untrained blades-men favored their own. The captain spoke: "Well done. The two of you are finished for the morning. More rounds of competition for the rest of you. Winners fight winners, losers fight losers. Keep at until I get you all sorted out." There were groans all around.

Marcus and his fallen opponent remained where they had fought. Marcus reached down and pulled on the boy-man's hand, raising him to his feet "You are good."

"But you are better," the boy-man said forlornly. "I hate losing. I've never lost before, well, not for a long time."

"That I believe. I have fought many, and now teach. I have rarely faced better."

His face brightened. "Really? You think I'm that good?"

Marcus gave a cynical laugh. "Oh please, don't patronize me. You *know* you're good. You hardly need me to say it. Now tell me. What is your name?"

"I'm Ivan. My friends call me *Ivan the Blade*. Or sometimes, just *Blade*, as in 'hey Blade, how yuh doin' today.' How about yourself, what's your name?"

"Marcus. As I told you, I teach edged weapons here at the military facility. I understand how they pulled me into this training. I'm young, but already a known blades-man. But tell me, Ivan, Blade, how is it that you come to be here?"

"Good question. I'm not sure I know myself. I've been in trouble a few times, so I guess the guardsmen know who I am. Those who don't know me personally probably know me by reputation. I was just relaxing with my friends when a man in a guardsman's uniform walked up, called me by name, and handed me an envelope. It had the King's crest on it. I was pretty impressed. It told me to be here, today. What is it everyone says? '*As the King commands*'. So here I am."

Marcus stood quietly, pondering, wondering if he should take Ivan into his confidence. The young man had an open, honest face, with intelligence in his eyes. Marcus mind-touched him and found no guile. He was clever and calculating, for sure, but he lacked the cynicism the under-class tended to grow into as they aged. Marcus followed his intuition. "Ivan, can you find it in yourself to trust me? As a friend and fellow blades-man?"

Ivan had a puzzled expression. "Trust you? Well, I guess so." He had a twinkle in his eye. "But the question is, can you trust *me*?"

Marcus gave him a grin and a nod in reply, then turned serious. "For some reason, yes I can. And believe me, violation of my trust would be harmful, even fatal, for us both. Probably faster for me than for you. But ultimately fatal nevertheless."

Ivan was slow to respond. "I take it this is pretty important? You're not joking, right?" He looked at the steely expression on Marcus' face and the resolve in his eyes. "Yeah, serious. What's it worth to me? I mean, it isn't like I work for free."

"You will work for the King, doing exactly what you were brought here to do. Of course, when I tell you *why* you were brought here, what they intend for you to do, you many have second thoughts. However, it is important that you continue. In addition to their pay, I will match it with coin of my own. Reveal this to anyone, and I will see you dead. Those terms good enough?"

Ivan gulped. "And you think you could take me, make me dead, just like that?"

Marcus gave an emotionless response, devoid of doubt. "Yes. So, do you want to work with me or not? And remember, even *mention* this little conversation to anyone and I make you dead." Marcus suddenly wondered if he could follow through on this spontaneous threat, or not. He reflected for a moment on Sinifir's evil plans and realized to his sudden horror, that yes, he could. What was he becoming, at the tender age of ten-and-five?

Ivan thought for a moment. "Do I have a choice? Looks like a lose-or-lose situation for me."

"No, not true. Work with me and you eventually win. I believe any other choice would be, as you say, a losing one."

"Then we be friends. Trusted friends. Life-death friends." He smiled and extended his hand. Marcus shook it. "Why do I think I've just gotten myself into a whole lot of trouble."

"Perhaps because you have. It all began with an envelope from the King. You are being recruited for the sole purpose of becoming a King's assassin."

CHAPTER

SEVEN

"**M**arcus! What in the world is that *awful* smell coming from your room! That stinks like animal dross, or worse!

Marcus shrugged. The odors of Kentuck's hovel had followed him home with the manuscripts. "Courtesy of Crazy Kentuck."

"Explain, please explain. But then, maybe you don't need to. These are the manuscripts he gave you, before he died?"

"Yes. And sorry about the smell. You know about his death?"

"Yes. One of the chapel mages came to tell me. Long ago the three of us were close friends. But that was many turns ago. Now please, have Marta get you some baking rout. Put it all over the pages. Rout absorbs odors quite well, hopefully enough to make this room tolerable. Rout. They use it in all the kitchens to keep the breads up and the smells down. Now, tell me. What have you discovered?"

Marcus looked over the top-most sheet. "Well, I'm just starting. There's a lot here. I looked through it briefly. It appears to be a lengthy cross-reference of words, *Turga* to *Kult*, and later, *Kult* to *Turga*. There are comments added here and there. Looks like when he wasn't completely sure of a *Kult* word, he added notes to that effect. If he had information of interest, he did the same. He had a good hand. It's fairly easy to read. If I can stand the smell."

Marcus returned the sheet he was handling to the top of the stack. He bundled them all together, rewrapped them in seal-skin, and put them into his chest. "And I must get that rout before this bundle of Kentuck's papers ruins my clothes."

His grandfather turned to leave.

"Wait, please. I have a question for you."

His grandfather paused and looked back. "Yes, of course. What do you want."

"Kentuck made reference to *tiemp*. He pronounced it tee-EMP. He said it meant 'time' in *Kult*. Have you ever heard that word before? Heard it used in any way?"

"*Tiemp*? No, can't say that I have. You sure that's the word he used?"

"Yes. He said something like '*tiemp* cannot be denied. It might be manipulated perhaps a little. But not denied. In the end it takes us all'."

"Time? Yes, I suppose times takes us all, in the end. But to *change* how time flows? That's why we called him *Kentuck the Crazy*. He was always spouting off foolish things like that."

And he called you Saul the Skeptic. Outlandish as it might be, Marcus was not in a rush to call Kentuck a crazy man. He had touched his mind. If anything, Kentuck was overly obsessed, but certainly not irrational. Marcus would explore *tiemp* on his own, without discussing it further with his grandfather.

Saul left, closing the door behind him, mostly to confine the smells to that single room.

Marcus retrieved Kentuck's manuscript bundle for the second time, determined to discover more about *tiemp*. The cross references were organized by initial letter. Finding at last the 'T's', he pored over the pages until he found *tiemp*. An entire paragraph had been dedicated to the word. Obviously Kentuck had made considerable effort analyzing its meaning and use. If Kentuck had understood correctly, *tiemp* meant much more than the simple measurement of passing events. There was a deeper relationship, tying the passing of time with the constant flow of *gift*. That flow could be quickened or slowed. Not for the entirely of creation, of course, but it could be manipulated for and about a mage with the power to do so. This much Kentuck had gleaned from the oldest of the manuscripts he had found. His final notation brought it into perspective.

Such ability, to manipulate time, comes to us by myth more than fact. However, like so many myths, it could well be based in truth. It seems consistent, given other myths of ancient mages who could appear and disappear at will. By manipulating time, or their presence within it, this seemingly impossible ability would be child's play. I have pondered this much, and believe this manipulation of tiemp *is indeed possible by a mage with appropriate endowment and power. Such a mage must be rare in deed, for there is nothing within known records that confirms such an ability.*

Marcus pondered what Kentuck had written. What type of endowment would this involve? It wasn't *earth-gift*. Or *mind-gift*, or any other type of *gift* he could imagine. If it existed, what would it be? *Time-gift*? Marcus put the manuscripts away for a second time and went to bed. Tomorrow was a seventh. His big task of the day would be to secure a plentiful supply of rout.

Marcus was beginning to doubt his sanity. All he could think of was learning *Kult*. Well, no, that wasn't quite true. He was obsessing over *tiemp*. Was he being pulled into the same circle-pool that had befallen *Kentuck the Crazy*? He hoped not.

The ranks of melee trainees had thinned over time. Several dropped out due to unintentional injury, others for a simple lack of skill. As to those injured, Marcus had his doubts. Remarkably, injuries seemed to befall the most unpopular and arrogant trainees. Their departures were neither mentioned nor regretted. To Marcus' surprise, one of those who survived the weeding was his old nemesis and first opponent. There was no way to describe him but by the word *thug*. But as he and Thomas (he had finally introduced himself) became better acquainted they became friends of a sort, background differences aside. For a big man – a very big man and strong – Thomas was quick. He was coarse in language and behavior. But behind his rough exterior lay a sharp, cunning and somewhat ruthless mind. He was intimidating in both appearance and fact. His one weakness, which Marcus exploited at will, was a total lack of subtlety. Marcus could anticipate his every move in hand-to-hand combat. And with mind-touch, Thomas was totally transparent. He did not know why he lost every confrontation with Marcus, but respected him for it. He not longer referred to Marcus as a *freckin' peacock*.

Eventually, each trainee had been issued a pair of daggers, long and thin and deadly and black. Melee training had then moved on to blade-casting. This was a skill with which few had experience, and Marcus alone with mastery. Casting with blades designed for that purpose was hard enough. Training began with them, but had eventually moved on to the casting of their daggers. The captain, Captain Morris by name, was relieved to have Marcus among his cadre and quick to ask him to lead instruction. Marcus had patiently demonstrated the several methods of holding and throwing a blade. The trick, he explained, was to cast the weapon point-first without causing it to tumble or turn in flight. It was a slow skill to learn, requiring much practice to be consistent, especially with the daggers. Marcus had mixed success in his teaching. The three who developed fastest were Ivan (to no surprise), the only woman in the group (Greta), and Thomas. As they gained proficiency, Marcus asked the three of them to help instruct the others. In doing so, he strengthened his connection with Ivan, cemented a friendship with Thomas, and gained a new friend in Greta. They would often eat together in the combat mess, discussing their melee comrades and sharing life stories. Marcus was the odd-man-out. His life of culture, education and formal training was totally foreign to the others. Each of the three came from the meanest of circumstances. Yet, they were becoming friends. Odd friends indeed. But friends nonetheless.

Greta was the quietest of the foursome and least inclined to speak of her personal journey. Marcus never pressed her on this, but tried to draw her out with patience and kindness. He listened to her opinions and gave genuine encouragement when he could. She responded, first with surprise and suspicion, then with increased openness.

She startled him one day, as training concluded, by grasped his arm. She pulled him into a confidential embrace, and asked him to stay and talk. They found a place to sit.

"Marcus," she said quietly. "I think you might be the only friend I have. Maybe the only friend I've ever had. You probably think I don't care about anyone but myself. But I do care for others. I care for Ivan. He's good, about as good as can be with a blade. But he isn't ruthless enough to go up against some of the men I've known. Thomas has a better chance. He's big enough to beat his way through most obstacles. You? You will always make it through. You have Ivan's quickness and Thomas' strength. And you are smarter than us all. And you are a nice person, besides. You will always have friends to watch your back."

"And you, Greta. How do you see yourself?"

"Survivor. Loner. Always a survivor and always alone. I will do almost anything to survive. You want me to steal? I will steal. Want me to lie and cheat. No problem. But there are two things I will not do. One of them is, I will not kill. Never again."

"And you see that as a problem?"

"I cannot ever be what they are training us to become. Neither can Ivan. Thomas? I'm not sure. He can kill, probably has. But Ivan and I could never become assassins."

"You have figured it out, then?"

"Duh. Tell me you haven't?"

Marcus nodded. "I know. These blades," he pointed at his daggers "are the tools of an assassin. They will confirm it when they make us swear unwavering allegiance to the King. And begin teaching potions and poisons. And forever silence, except among ourselves. Assassins always work alone and in the dark. It is an evil thing."

"And you could do it, become an assassin?"

Marcus thought how to answer. He had never considered Greta as a co-conspirator. But here she was, essentially calling his hand. His mind-touch revealed nothing more than profound sadness. "Before I answer, I want to know more about you. I have my own agenda, true. But it is one that I am unwilling to share without knowing you better."

Greta seemed to understand. She signed, again with great sadness. "My story is not so different than others who are poorly born. My father abandoned my mother when I was but a babe. In desperation she turned to the flesh trade. My early life was a constant coming and going of boys and men. When the flower of youth had been beaten away, all too often by the feet and fists of her customers, our lives fell into even deeper despair. She moved in with one of her last lovers. She knew he had an eye for me – I was but a hand and two then – but she was willing to sacrifice me for regular food and a roof over her head. I knew he was coming for me, and I resolved not to be taken, to fall into the miserable life shown me by my mother. So when he came..." Greta stopped, wiping tears from her eyes. "When he came for me, I was ready. I cut him. I cut him from neck to groin. I poured all the sadness, the anger, the disgust – everything – I poured it all into my attack. There was blood everywhere, My mother screamed, calling me names I cannot bear to recall, let alone repeat. She didn't care about me, only about him. He who had abused and degraded her time and time again in the vilest of ways, wanted to do the same to me." The tears had stopped, replaced by steel, *old-steel*, in her voice. "So I ran, with his blood and gore on my hands. I resolved then that I would never kill again. Nor would I ever fall to the level of my mother. Anything else, to survive? No problem. Lie? Cheat? Steal? Assault? Again, no problem. But I've never been bedded. And I have never killed again. I learned to protect myself, as you have had ample proof. Life has been hard, Marcus, and there has been no one to extend care or concern. Until maybe now. Maybe here. For the first time, I'm thinking of you as a friend. And that I am safe with you at my back. And I would not see harm come to these other two. Is there anything else you need to know?"

Marcus shook his head. There were tears in his own eyes. "I tell you, so you know now and not later. I am heir to the Lord High-mage, Saul Aurelius. In time, I will stand next to the King in both protection and counsel. You ask if I could kill? I have faced the prospect and believe I could. If I had to choose between life and death, protect my own life or that of the King of Iber? Yes, I could kill. Without hesitation. But never as an assassin. Never at the direction or command of another. And like you, bedding is for married folk and below the dignity of any other relationship."

They seemed to have reached an end of the conversation. Marcus began another. "What do you know of mages?"

"Mages are evil, They tap an unholy power prohibited by the *fata* themselves."

"What about health-mages?"

"I suppose that might be an exception. But all other mages are bad."

"Greta, only the ignorant so believe. Mage-power is called *gift*. It is *gift* that gives life to all livings things, animal or plant. Mages simply have access to a greater portion of that life force. It is not prohibited. Nor is it bad. Although it can become corrupted and used for evil rather than good. My family, for over four-hand generations, well over a hand-fist of turns, has stood by the kings and queens of Iber, accessing *gift* for their protection and counsel.

Marcus continued, with a far-away gaze. "But there has arisen a new mage, not of my family's line. He competes for the attention of the King. His *gift* is that of a mind-mage, a dangerous *gift* where he is able to touch and manipulate the thoughts of others. And thereby influence their actions. His name is *Sinifir*. It is a name you must remember. He is what we call a *dark* mage, a man whose *gift* has become twisted into a pursuit of wealth and power. Human life means nothing to him, and war is the coin of his ambition." Marcus turned to face Greta. "We are not being trained to be assassins for the King, but to be the secret, destroying hand of Sinifir in his grasp for power and wealth. I have told this to Ivan, and now I disclose it to you. The time is not yet come, but soon will, when we must rise up and bring an end to Sinifir. And to his willing accomplice, Prince Stephen. Both are ambitious, besot with an evil beyond redemption. Will you work with me to prevent this from happening?"

Greta gave a solemn nod. "Yes, I will."

The die had been cast. For good or ill, Marcus had two co-conspirators. Three if he included Princess Katrina.

Melee training finally progressed to its eponym. Marcus did not like hand-to-hand combat. To him, it was nothing short of brawling. There were formalized styles of wrestling and hand-striking,, true. But melee was far removed from any such elegance. You fought to win. You fought to live. There were no niceties. Only survival, or not.

Marcus had but little prior training in hand-to-hand, even less interest in learning more. His agility, fitness and strength guaranteed him some success. Mind-touch was but a small advantage against the bigger men, men such as Thomas. With mind-touch he might anticipate moves and avoid them. But only temporarily. Eventually he would be cornered and seized.

Thereafter, he had scant hope of escape. He decided he would provide a token, a modicum, of challenge in each confrontation. But would be content to lose with as much honor as losing well could provide. He would count it a solid success if he could escape with but minor injury. Marcus counseled Ivan the same. But Ivan was slow to understand. He was even slower to agree.

In this part of the course, advantage went to the un-trained. These understood fighting, life or death, without regard to discipline or dignity. Greta emerged as one of the deadliest. She was the only one to best Thomas, though in a real fight, both would certainly have been badly injured. Fortunately, combatants wore protective gear over the most susceptible anatomy: throat, groin and head. But arms and legs were fair game.

Captain Morris warned, and warned often, that aggression was expected, cruelty was not. "It is not in our interest to have anyone disabled. Stop when your opponent concedes. And to you *losers*, concede immediately when you know you have lost, or are about to lose. This is about learning, not winning." No one believed it less than Captain Morris himself. Grudges had developed over time. Melee was where they would be settled. Marcus had been a consistent winner during blade training, but always gracious in victory. He was now a target to be beaten, not one to be defeated. There was a clear difference.

Ivan had not been so wise. Marcus feared for him, and for good reason. Ivan was a bit shorter and thinner than Marcus and had strutted his victories like the 'freckin' peacock' Thomas had so colorfully described him those many seven-days before. Retribution was soon in coming. Ivan managed to survive several encounters with 'trained' members of the cadre. He hadn't won, but his opponents were civilized enough to respect his concessions. The inevitable end came against a large untrained man by the name of Louton. Ivan dodged and weaved, using his speed and agility to his advantage. He made Louton look bad in the process. But Marcus knew that Ivan had no offense to bring against his opponent. The fight would not, could not, conclude in a protracted draw. Louton was a vain man with an easily-aroused temper. He was always aching for retaliation and would never accept such a end.

Louton finally caught Ivan across the throat with an outstretched arm. He had been scrambling desperately to evade, and his quickness worked against him. One moment he was moving, next flying in a back-flip, head-first, to the arena sand. Louton was on him in a moment, throwing his full weight into a kick that lifted Ivan well off the ground. There was a sickening *crack* of broken ribs. Ivan went immediately into a pallor of pain and shock.

Marcus had been watching intently and leapt quickly to his feet, preventing Louton from striking again. Captain Morris rushed in as well, blanching at the injuries Ivan had sustained. He gave Louton a fierce stare. "I told you, Louton, I told *everyone*, no serious injuries. What part of that did you *not* understand?"

Louton shrugged, turned, and walked away. He didn't care. The debt between him and Ivan had been settled.

Serious injuries, though infrequent, were not unknown. Marcus held Ivan's hand and encouraged him to lie still. His labored breathing and blood-flecked spittle were sure evidence of a pierced lung. Two men rushed through the crowd and threw a stretcher on the sand. Marcus helped them lift Ivan gently and carry him to the dispensary. A healer-mage was usually on duty. Fortunately, for Ivan, such was the case today.

There was little that Marcus could do for his friend, except to stay by his side and provide what little comfort he could. The health-mage placed his hands over Ivan's bruising wound, and began to mentally probe the injury. Ivan gave an involuntary groan. Out of both curiosity and habit, Marcus used mind-touch to follow the mage's actions.

The process was both gruesome and fascinating. The mage could sense, almost *see*, the internal injuries. There were three broken ribs, torn cartilage, and a pierced lung. Marcus felt the mage tug mentally on the offending rib. Then tug again, without success.

He lacked power in *gift* to pull the rib free. In desperation, Marcus *pushed* some of his own *gift* into both Ivan and the mage. The mage gave a small jolt of surprise.

"Please," pleaded Marcus, "please, you must try again."

This time, with Marcus pushing the power of additional *gift* into the effort, the rib came free and slipped into its proper place, more or less. The mage then proceeded to repair the pierced lung by pulling flesh over flesh and sealing the wound shut. Ivan's breathing immediately became less labored. The mage then moved the three ribs to their proper position and knitted the bones together in a temporary repair. With Marcus' help, they swathed Ivan's chest and ribs in multiple layers of wide bandage. When done, the mage gave Ivan a sip of brown liquid. Almost immediately, he lapsed into unconsciousness.

"A sleeping draught. Quite strong. He will be out for quite a while. You going to stay with him, make sure there are no complications? You'll call me if there are?"

Marcus nodded in replay. "Yes, he's a friend. But I will need to let Captain Morris know."

"I think he knows where you are. But I'm going that way to return the stretcher. The way you boys are going at it, you'll likely need it again soon enough. I'll make sure Captain Morris knows where you are." He was quiet for a moment. "I have, uh, a question for you. Are you a mage?"

Marcus nodded.

"I thought so. I felt you push *gift* both into him and me. I didn't know that was possible." He nodded toward the sleeping Ivan. "I'm passable as a health-mage, but not that strong. Not that powerful. I know what has to be done. I can *see* it. But I don't have enough *gift* to do much about it. You saw I couldn't pull his rib free. And I was trying as hard as I possibly could, with all my power of *gift*. Then you stepped in and together we got it out. And knitted flesh and bone together. I am sure your friend would have otherwise bled out from the inside, slowly strangled by his own blood. I've seen it often enough. Not an easy way to die." With that, he left with the stretcher across his shoulders.

Marcus pulled a chair over to Ivan's bed. *So that is what healing is all about. The mage showed me how to look inside, how to mend. Could I do it by myself, if I had to? Would that make me a health-mage? Fata bless me, I hope I never have to find out. And I didn't realize it was that easy to cast* gift *into another. There is much to think about.* Marcus was content to sit quietly and monitor Ivan's breathing. It held steady. Marcus pushed a bit more *gift* into him and gradually his color returned. It grew late in the day. Melee would be ending soon, if not over already. He started, feeling the presence of another. Standing beside him was Greta.

"The stupid grout. Is he going to live?"

"Looks like. He's on the mend."

She pulled up another chair, sighed, and sat. "It looked pretty bad. Goodness, it *sounded* bad. Ribs?"

"Three, one through a lung."

"So I heard. The health mage gave Captain Morris a full account and I sneaked a listen. Mage said you helped pull him through. I don't think Captain Morris realized you were a mage."

"And now everyone knows?"

"Maybe, maybe not. I was the only one standing by. Captain Morris knows it would be bad for you if the others found out. He asked the healer to remain silent, so it might not get around."

"Well, we can hope. And that's about all, hope."

"Yeah. So go on home, Marcus, you've done what you can. It's my turn now. Stupid kid that he is, he's still a friend."

"At least you see him that way. Now there's two."

Greta gave him a puzzled look.

"Friends, Greta, friends. Now you've got two of us."

"May the *fata* spare me!"

CHAPTER
EIGHT

Marcus was tired when he got home. He and his grandfather shared the evening meal and were about to retire to their respective rooms. Marcus hesitated, then asked if they might remain to visit a bit.

"Of course, son, what's on your mind?"

"I have a question about *gift*. It should be a simple one. Today, in melee, my friend Ivan got hurt quite badly. He was viciously kicked by a much larger man and suffered some broken ribs and a punctured lung."

"Oh my. That is serious. Did he die?"

"No, and that's what I want to talk to you about. We got him to the dispensary and fortunately, a health-mage was on duty. He could see inside and knew what the problem was, but didn't have enough *gift* power to make the repairs."

"Not that unusual. Few health-mages could have fixed a problem that big."

"Really? I thought health-mages could fix all kinds of problems."

"It's easy to over-estimate *gift* power in others, Marcus. It's a bit like mind-touch. Mind-mages can reach out and influence the thoughts of others. But it's more of a nudge than a shove. They can't actually *read* someone's mind. You have begun reading the annals that speak of past mages, the ones that made history. They are mentioned because they were extraordinarily powerful. Read enough, and you are left with the impression that their level of power is common. It isn't. Each generation produces only a few worth mentioning. In all likelihood, your health-mage was somewhat above the average. But you said your friend is recovering? That's good."

"Yes, and that is what I wanted to talk to you about. Not that he's recovering, but how it came to be. Is it possible to cast pure *gift*? I mean, I know *gift* can influence other things. I can move air, I can cast flame. I can create light. and I can direct arrows and bolts and spears to a target..."

Saul interrupted. "Wait! You said you could make arrows and such change direction in flight?"

"Well, yes. Is that a surprise? I thought any earth-mage could do that."

"Marcus, it's one thing to push a pencil off a table, or move a feather across the room. But the amount of *gift* to do so is proportional to weight and momentum. It would take a tremendous amount of *gift* power to move a heavy object, say a spear, in its flight. Are you *sure* you can do this, that it's not just an illusion?"

Marcus shrugged. "It's real, and, yes. I do it all the time. Well, not all the time. I keep it quiet, discrete, as you instructed. But I've never considered it a big matter. You're saying that it's uncommon?"

"Much so." Saul gave a bewildered shake of his head. "We will need to talk more of this, later. Now, back to your question. You wanted to know if a mage could cast pure *gift*? Why do you ask?"

"Well, during the operation, when I sensed the health-mage didn't have enough *gift-power* to save my friend, I pushed some of my *gift* to him. He then had enough to pull the rib from my friend's lung and patch up the tissues and bones. He was surprised he could do that, and deduced that I had helped. He had never seen or heard of anyone receiving *gift* from someone else, so I thought to ask you if what I did was common or not."

Saul was quiet for several moments, thinking. "Marcus, there are many things about *gift* that I do not know. I have not been as studious as, say, your late friend Kentuck. He would certainly know more. But to answer your question, no. I don't know of any mage able to share or cast pure *gift*. I guess the only thing that comes close is when two mages become *paired*, and that is rare enough."

"Paired? What is that?"

"Like I said, it's rare, so it's unlikely you've heard of it. You had a great-great, let's see, great-great-grand-uncle and aunt, on your father's side, that were paired. That would have been my grand-father's great uncle and aunt. I think I got the right number of 'greats' in there. Anyway, the two of them were very close as husband and wife, and eventually went through a ceremony which joined their life-forces. It involved a word of power. I don't know what the word was, but Kentuck's cross-reference probably has it. Look under 'pairing'. In any case, I knew them both when I was a very young mage. They were old at the time, the last of their generation by a goodly number of turns. I was curious, and asked them what it meant to be *paired*. They said they were always very close, as if they had similar *gift*. Finally they reached a point where they wanted a closer tie, a life-binding."

"A life-binding? What's that? Is it stronger than marriage?"

"Yes, *much* stronger than marriage. Marriage is a contract, such as 'till death do us part'. A life-binding combines two life forces together as one. Such bonding cannot be broken, even in death. As I understand it, if one dies, the shock of separation, the return of life-force to the earth, takes the other as well. They pass into the great unknown together, still as one. At least that's what they said. Such life- and *gift*-bonding goes by the common name of *mage-marriage*. I guess I shouldn't say the 'common name', as it isn't at all common. It's uncommon for two reasons. First,, it can only be done with two mages of considerable *gift*. And two, those two *gifts* must be highly compatible. Otherwise, no binding can occur, words of power notwithstanding."

"What do you mean, *compatible*?"

"Questions. One always leads to another! We always say that each individual is unique in his or her *gift*. It's true, for all I know. But it doesn't mean there cannot be two people with *similar gift*. Think of it like, oh, personality. No two people are the same. But there are people that get along together better than others. Same ideas about life, same way of interpreting people and events. Those sorts of things. People like that are attracted to each other. People of similar *gift* feel drawn to each other in much the same way. The closer the similarity, the stronger the attraction. Getting back to your original question. Let's see, what was it? Oh yes, can a person cast pure *gift*? That's how I got sidetracked by *pairing*. What they said was that when their life-forces were merged, the stronger of the two (the wife, in their case) made a *gift-cast*– that was the way they described it – to the other. The two strengths merged and quickly equalized Thereafter, each had access to the full power of the two combined. Not only that, together they had a bit more *gift* than the sum of two before pairing."

"Did they also share their particular endowments, after pairing?"

"You mean, if an earth-mage paired with a health-mage, would the first become a health-mage also, and vice-versa?"

"Yes, that's what I wondered."

"I don't know. I asked them the same question and they were a big careful in how they answered. I got the impression they communicated on a different level than mere speech. And it was some things they had agreed to keep secret. They finally answered me by saying 'we are aware of each other's endowment'."

"Thank you. I guess you answered my question. Though I think I have a hand-fist more to ponder. Good night. I have some reading to do! By the way, I bought a box of rout. You were right. I think it's made Kentuck's manuscripts a bit more tolerable."

Saul nodded, shuddered, and muttered in a low voice. "New moon coming, *fata* spare us." He walked to his room and shut the door.

Marcus stared after his grandfather. Yes, the nights were growing darker as the moon slowly regressed across the sky, night-by-night. In a few days it would only be visible for a short time after sunset as a waning crescent. Marcus had noticed, on many prior occasions, his grandfather's wary regard for new moons. He often made a foreboding comment on the same, as he had tonight. Marcus had no idea why, as he actually found new moons to be oddly invigorating. He had mentioned as much to his grandfather several times, mostly as a spiteful rejoinder to his malaise. To such, his grandfather would always respond with something of the form 'Yes, and may the *fata* spare us all'.

Marcus closed the door after entering, cast flame to light the several candles in the room, and retrieved Kentuck's dictionary (that's what he had begun calling it) from the chest where he kept it. He searched through the P's until finding the reference for *pairing*.

Pairing is a semi-rare ceremony performed between two powerful mages of similar gift. They must also have a strong affinity for, and commitment to, each other. Pairing, however, is a weak description of their condition. It is better described as a binding of life-forces. In a pairing, each person speaks the word Alpare – all-PAR-ay, with the intent of binding. Life forces are exchanged and balanced. For pairing to occur, the individuals must be in physical contact, or the life forces cannot be passed. Pairing is not to be undertaken lightly, for life forces once merged in this way cannot be separated, even by death. For as the life-force of one is returned to the earth from whence it came, it generally pulls the life force of the other to the same destination. Those who have paired, by the few accounts that exist, combine each other's power in gift.

Endowments remain separate. The melding of life-force creates a single mind in which emotions and even thoughts are said to be shared. By all accounts, pairing is a matter of choice. But there is myth that two people of identical gift are drawn together by the compelling attraction of the two gifts to merge as one. If resisted, the stronger of the two will actually pull the life-force from the other. In such a case, pairing would be the only way for the weaker to survive.

Marcus looked for any references for *gift-casting* but found nothing of use.

Melee was subdued. Everyone was surprised by Ivan's arrival at the mid-day meal two days after his injuries. He walked slowly and sat carefully, unable to do more than observe the day's instruction and subsequent contests. Marcus and Greta spoke encouraging words to him. Even Thomas came by to briefly welcome his return. Louton gave Ivan no notice whatsoever.

This became a pattern that continued for the next four and a half seven-days. Ivan was clearly well-healed, but only reluctantly engaged others in combat. He was equally gracious in his rare victories and frequent defeats. Gone were the bravado and arrogance, replaced with deference and respect. It was noticed and appreciated. The others in the cadre began to speak kindly in return, Louton being the exception.

Marcus stood in the arena sand, awaiting his opponent. The sand was warm and he enjoyed letting it sift through his curled toes. Strangely, he looked forward to the approaching grapple. There was a growing feeling of vitality within him. He found himself reaching out to embrace it. His last thoughts were *this is just like casting* gift, *but in the opposite direction. It is wonderful. Wonderful! Please, don't stop.*

The surge in *gift* was sudden and overwhelming. Marcus was pitched to the ground, arms and legs stretched out to their fullest. He lost consciousness, open eyes staring into nothingness. His skin reddened as if burnt. His breathing became shallow and labored. He convulsed, spasms tearing through his body. His stomach and bowels voided. He began to thrash. His hands and feet frantically churned the sand.

Marcus awoke in the castle dispensary. Unlike the meager dispensary in the barracks, this was clean and white, with a faint aroma of antiseptic camphor in the air. Every part of his body was burned, but more so those areas that had touched the sand. It was as if he had spent much too much unprotected time in the mid-day sun, but worse. He struggled to sit up, finding in doing so he became dizzy and nauseous. There was a bowl at his arm. He took it and voided his stomach, though only a bitter fluid came forth. His bones and ligaments ached with every movement he made. Without doubt, he had never been so ill. And he had no understanding of *why*. One moment he felt well, even better than mere 'well'. Then, the next moment he had been overwhelmed by *something* unknown. It was that *something* that made no sense to him whatever. He lay back down, feeling some relief, and lapsed into sleep. When he awoke again, his grandfather quietly sat in a chair at the foot of the bed.

"*Fata* be praised, the boy lives!" Marcus heard his grandfather exclaim.

The health mages offered no explanation for Marcus' malady. Sunstroke? Food poisoning? Stress reaction? The one thing they agreed upon, was that he had no internal problems, only damage to his skin. And it was nothing worse than a very bad sun-burn.

Saul knew otherwise, but he kept it to himself. After one more day in the dispensary, Marcus was discharged and returned home. His skin was peeling and itching, the oils they provided gave much relief. The following day was a seventh. Marcus was content to rest and eat. He had a voracious appetite and slowly returned to his normal vigor. There was, however, a marked change in his level of *gift*. He had made a small flame-cast to light his candles. But to his surprise, the candles completely melted. He thought to mention this to his grandfather, but forbore.

The next morning, a first-day, he returned to melee. Captain Morris announced an end to training on the up-coming sixth-day. "There is someone who would like to meet each of you. He is a counselor to the King. He and the King share a keen interest in your development. He would like to see a demonstration of your individual abilities. I trust you will do well, so let's practice diligently in preparation."

Marcus knew immediately he spoke of Sinifir. He would need to warn Ivan, Greta and Thomas. But for now, there was training.

Marcus faced off against Louton, and did a light mind-touch to anticipate his moves. To Marcus' surprise, Louton grabbed his head, screamed, and dropped to his knees. Marcus withdrew the mind-touch, and Louton recovered. He continued to grasp his head and whimper, but obviously the pain had subsided. Marcus knew he had caused this, but did not comprehend how. The understanding burst into clarity. Like the destroyed candles, his power in *gift* had greatly expanded and strengthened through his recent ordeal. He would ask grandfather about this. And perhaps get a useful answer? Marcus went through the rest of the day without accessing his *gift* in any intentional way.

Marcus raised the question after dinner. "Is it possible, grandfather, that what I went through the last few days has affected my *gift* power in some way?"

"Why do you ask?"

"Well, when I went to light my candle last night, as I always do, I melted it down to a puddle of wax." He didn't want to tell his grandfather anything specific about mind-touch. "And today, when I went to use a little bit of *gift* in melee training, the effect was much, much greater than I expected."

Saul let out a sigh. "Well, yes, there is a possibility. But it's hard to know if the effects will be temporary or permanent. As you have been taught, and probably read, *gift* exists everywhere. But what is *not* taught is that a stream of it flows through the earth. The flow is constant, always present. And it seems to follow certain paths, almost like rivers do on the surface."

Marcus had read about this in the Chronicles, of course. He thought about what Kentuck had written, that the flow of *gift* and the flow of *time* were related.

Saul continued. "But at the exact end of the lunar cycle, when the sun and moon are together pulling on the earth, that flow of *gift* is drawn close to the surface. At the precise moment of greatest attraction, when the sun and moon are exactly aligned, there is a pulse, or surge, of *gift* power, that flows around the earth. This is greater in some cycles than in others. And day-time passings tend to be stronger than those that occur at night, in my experience. It is during the *gift* surge that strange and unexpected manifestations of *gift* can occur. That's why you always hear me muttering at the time of new moons. Usually, I only feel it if I am standing on the ground. It causes me to feel, well, invigorated. And on rare occasions, my feet itch. My guess is that you, with greater *gift* than I, fell victim to one of these surges and suffered what is called *gift sickness*. It is much like the first time you cast flame. Simply explained, a four-day ago you were exposed to more *gift* than your body could withstand. *Gift* sickness can be fatal if it overwhelms the life force of the sufferer. And by the way, that's how rogue mages are put down."

Marcus was shocked: "Rogue mages, being put down? What do you mean with that?"

"Well, it's a dark thing and it happens very rarely, perhaps once or twice a generation, sometime less. As you know, *gift* can be used for evil instead of good, Sinifir being a prime example. How do you destroy a mage as he? I suppose an arrow or bolt or spear might do it. But truly great mages gain a sense of an impending attack of that sort, almost like an extra sense. And will take appropriate action to prevent or avoid it. In such cases, a rogue mage can only be taken down, defeated, killed, whatever, by a more powerful mage, or more likely a group of mages collectively, with sufficient power to overcome the rogue's defenses. The mage or mages attack the rogue with their particular powers, *earth-gift, mind-gift, health-gift* for example, until the rogue's life-force is overwhelmed and he is destroyed. Think of it this way. Withdraw life-force, *gift* if you would rather, and a person dies. Likewise, too much life force all at one time and the same happens. The person dies of *gift-sickness*."

"That must be quite a spectacle."

"And extremely dangerous. In the confusion of casting and the swirling of *gift* power, it's easy for an attacking mage to lose awareness of his own *gift* levels. He could become so depleted of life-force that he also dies in the process. Of course, if the rogue mage is dangerous enough, attacking mages might intentionally surrender their entire life-force to defeat him."

"How is it that you know so much about this, if it's as rare as you say it is?"

"It is called *gift-silencing* and is something every high-mage is taught. I was taught of it by my father shortly before his passing, when he knew I would become the next Lord High-mage. But I've gotten off-track a bit. You asked about your apparent new strength in *gift*. Your question has to do with how *all* mages grow in *gift-power*. As mages grow older, and *if* they access their *endowments* on a regular basis, their *gift-power* increases. Much like a muscle grows stronger through repeated exercise. Or a better example might be a goat's bladder. If you close off one end and blow in to the other, it fills with air and expands. When you release the air, the bladder returns to its previous size, almost. Actually, it is just a little bit bigger. If you repeat the process, the bladder can stretch to a larger size, permanently. So what I think happened, at the new-moon surge of *gift*, you were filled with so much power that it nearly overwhelmed your life force. With your reservoir of *gift* over-filled, as it is now, your normal use of *gift* is greatly magnified. But not to worry, once your reservoir goes back down, it will be much as before. However, your capacity to absorb *gift*, the amount you can hold safely, is probably slightly greater than before. Does this make sense?"

Marcus nodded. "I understand. So for a while I have to be very careful using any form of *gift*. How long does it take to return to normal? It seems to me that if I don't use *gift*, then I will never draw down its power to where it was before."

"Well, you are partly right. Life itself consumes *gift*. There is a normal flow of *gift* from the earth that fairly evenly balances what we use. Otherwise, everyone would quickly die. You might think of *aging* as the gradual decline of the level of life-force a person holds. In your case, the amount of *gift* you currently have, versus the amount of *gift* that would normally flow to you, is quite different. I believe this difference will cause your extra *gift* to trickle back to the earth. So in time you are back to where you were, more or less. However, you will probably be a bit stronger, given the over-all increase in your capacity to hold *gift*. As to the time for this to happen? Your guess is as good as mine."

Marcus thanked his grandfather and went to his room. It was growing late and he had become tired. Nevertheless, sleep did not come easily. He lay awake until much past mid-night pondering the information his grandfather had shared.

The next day, a second-day, Marcus invited Ivan, Greta and Thomas to take mid-day meal together. Once they were seated and the meal consumed, he explained why he wanted to meet. "Thomas, we haven't spoken much to you about our concerns. But suffice it to say that the mage who wants to interview us is not a good man. He is what we call a *dark mage*. He is strong in *gift* and his particular ability is to touch and influence the minds of others. He is called a *mind-mage*. These can be become very dangerous, but *only if* they become obsessed with an ambition for power and wealth. Such is the case of Sinifir, the mage Captain Morris spoke of this morning. Making matters worse, he has influenced the King, an otherwise good man, to lust for those same things. Sinifir will lead the King, and therefore the Kingdom of Iber, to war to achieve his ends. This melee training will be used by Sinifir to create a cadre of assassins to further his ambitions."

"Well, that brings some t'ings together. Once we got the daggers, I know'd we would be up to mischief. Assassins? Yeah, that's what I figger'd out too. You be a mage as well, like Sinifir?"

"Well, I'm a mage, but not a *mind*-mage. And by the *fata, not* like Sinifir. I guess that was pretty obvious, that I'm a mage?"

"Ever'one knows you be diff'rent in some way. Bein' a mage makes sense, seein' what you did for Ivan here. It's what I figger'd you to be, maybe some kinda health-mage. I'm settled widdit either way. What are we supposed to do about this Sinifir guy?"

"He cannot read your mind but he can influence your thoughts. Especially if he can feed your personal desires. I think he mostly wants to get a taste of what we are individually able to do. And where we have weaknesses he can exploit. He probably won't need more than three or four assassins to do his dark and dirty work. In fact, I would think just a few could make a world of difference. Further, I think the three of you are prime candidates, along with Louton. If you are selected, Sinifir will likely invite you, or compel you, to a 'secret meeting' where you will swear allegiance to him and the King. After that, you would probably be taught the finer tools of an assassin. Things like potions and poisons."

Greta and Ivan had sat silently throughout the discussion. "Well, for one, I could never become an assassin, you know that," Greta said firmly.

Ivan: "Nor I. Thomas, what about you."

"You know I'm not a good person. I've killed a few men. But only if they needed killin', yuh understand. I'm with you, don't think I could kill just for the sake of killin'."

Marcus: "Trouble with a mind-mage, Thomas, is that he will convince you that the person you've been sent to eliminate *is* one of those 'needing' folks, whether he be or not."

It was time to return to training. They agreed to meet again on fourth-day.

By fourth-day, Marcus could tell his *gift-power* had declined. It was still stronger than usual, but was becoming manageable. He could light a candle without burning down his room, and he could use mind-touch without causing pain to the intended. He was much relieved. Over lunch, he suggested a strategy for dealing with Sinifir: "He will watch us in combat, so we must do our best. He will then want to talk to us individually. Be polite. He holds a high position and is accustomed to the deference of others. As you speak to him, he is likely to probe your mind and attempt to implant certain thoughts and ideas. When you feel this happening – and if you are looking for it you will know when it happens – focus away from him. Personally, I want to build a barrier between him and me. So I'm going to fix a clear thought of one of the castle walls in my mind. Don't get too nervous. I know how it works and I can give you a taste of how it will be. Are you willing?"

They all nodded, a bit of worry in their faces. "Now, Greta. You try it first." Marcus touched her mind and cast a thought of food, a rich venison stew. He saw her eyes lift, and with a smile she licked her lips. "So how was it?"

"Venison stew. I want some. Now!" She thought for a moment. "By the *fata* themselves, that is persuasive."

"Now let's try again, but this time, think of a wall." Marcus repeated the mind-touch, thinking this time on a rich sweat-mead. "How did you do?"

"I don't know. I just kept thinking of a wall, as you suggested."

"Excellent! Thomas, you ready?"

When Marcus was finished with Thomas and Ivan, it was time to return to training. He had done what he could. He hoped it would be enough.

Sixth-day arrived, the cadre meeting time with Sinifir was scheduled for mid-morning. Clearly, it was a big event for Captain Morris. Vestments were ready and waiting for all hand and two trainees. The leather breaches went to the knee. Light, heel-less boots, finely twined rope-weed shirts, leather jerkins and greaves completed their attire. The shirts were white, the leathers were a dull brown in color but highly polished. Everything appeared new. Each pile of clothing was labeled with a name and careful preparations had been made for size and fit. Trainees paired up to get the greaves properly laced. When finished, they attached their daggers to belts and slung a quiver of bolts over the right shoulder. A short cross-bow went over the left, as directed by Captain Morris. He then had everyone stand at attention for an inspection. Adjustments were made as necessary. For the trainees with military experience, this was nothing out of the ordinary. But for those without, the close inspection and attention to detail produced compliance, but with a roll of the eyes.

Captain Morris brought everyone back to attention. "Let me tell you what I have been told about today's events. First, I want to emphasize how serious and important this is to our entire training program. The high-mage who will be coming is a direct representative of the King himself. He will report our development directly to him. Everyone understand this?" He waited for an acknowledgement. "That being the case, we need to be on our best behavior. No joking, no laughing. The high-mage will be speaking to each of you. When he does, you answer *respectfully* using his title of Lord. As in, 'yes, m'lord'. Or 'no, m'lord'. Nothing more, unless he asks you *specifically* for something else. If he does, *think before answering!* And answer in as few words as possible. Do you understand this? Oh, and one more thing. Do not ever look him directly in the eye. Such would be a sign of disrespect." Again he waited for a murmured reply. "Now, on to the reason for the review. He has asked for a simple demonstration of your prowess in arms. This will be blade and cross-bow skills only, no melee. Thankfully. We do not want to mess up your pretty new vestments."

There were a few chuckles, which Captain Morris silenced with a glare.

"Blade work will involve dagger casting only, no one-on-one. On a signal, which I shall give, you will each withdraw a dagger, the longer one, and cast it at a designated target. He and I will be taking note of your collective and *individual* accuracy and speed. *Please* do not miss the target or have your blade fail to stay embedded. Got it?" Again, he waited for understanding. "Next is skill in cross-bow. Same process. At my command, retrieve the weapon, load it, and cast at the target on the left. Same as before. Focus on speed and accuracy. Are there any questions?" There were none.

"I'm not positive what comes next, but it is possible he will invite you to individually step forward. Again, and remember well, no eye contact unless he specifically asks you to look at him. Which I assure you, will be unlikely. And as I told you before, answer his questions thoughtfully but briefly. Any more questions?" He didn't wait for a reply. "Good. Then be at ease. Lord Sinifir should be here shortly."

Marcus had time to reflect on his fellow trainees. Including himself there were twelve, five 'trained' and seven 'untrained'.

Eljay (trained). Mostly a grunt-soldier, but well-built and intelligent. Marcus thought of him as 'solid' in all skills, remarkable in none. Dependable. He had been trained to follow orders without question.

Winston (trained). Not literally a twin to Eljay, but close enough. He came out of the cavalry side of the military and was a bit more lean and agile. Good with cross-bow. Like Eljay, he was an order-follower.

Abden (trained). Everyone called him "Abs". Tall and sinewy. He came from the archers, so his casting skills were excellent. His height worked against him in melee, as his larger and more muscular opponents would bind him in his own arms and legs. He was perhaps the nicest of the combatants. Although he was trained to follow orders, Marcus doubted he would obey a command to kill without a clear justification. No, he would not make it as an assassin.

Lindon (last of the trained). Another 'grunt' soldier. He had never spoken much of his pre-military life. Marcus suspected a criminal background of some sort, as he was more violent and aggressive than necessary. As a natural bully, he obviously enjoyed melee, pushing the limits of pain even after an opponent conceded. He was second largest of the trainees, exceeded only by Thomas in size and strength. Marcus had avoided him as often as possible in melee. When they were matched, he had had to resort to mind-touch to persuade a release before injury. Marcus had never defeated him in melee. He was definitely assassin material.

Carlos (untrained). Thief. And like most thieves, he had a total disregard for anyone or anything other than himself. Unliked by others, he suffered accordingly in melee. He tended to held grudges. Good in blades, mediocre in everything else. Of all the trainees, Marcus placed him in the two or three top candidates for assassin.

Matthew (Matt, untrained). Another thief, but unlike Carlos, a happy thief. Marcos thought he had stolen as much for the excitement of it as the desire for plunder. He was more social, often telling riotous jokes and pulling occasional pranks. These had an undercurrent of meanness, though. And Marcus could easily imagine Matt as a double-faced assassin: pleasant and social on one hand, unsuspected but deadly on the other. He was the type to use poisons first, weapons only if necessary. He would become an assassin to be feared.

Camden (untrained). He never directly spoke of his background. But the hints he dropped screamed 'thief', a bandit through and through. He stole for coin, with neither remorse nor concern for the consequences to others. Without conscience, he would jump at the chance to become an assassin. If the price were right. And he would be very affordable.

The other three were well known by Marcus. Louton the cruel. Thomas, ruffian and giant, but a man with hidden intelligence and conscience. Greta, the lethal loner. And finally, Ivan, deadly with blade and quiet. And fortunately, a friend.

Marcus wondered how each with fare under the influence and persuasion of a mind-mage of Sinifir's strength. He did not have long to wait.

Sinifir came sweeping into the arena and ascended the small dais erected for the occasion. Marcus kept his head bowed, but stole a glance through his brows. Sinifir wore a hooded black robe (*how appropriate, thought Marcus*) with billowing sleeves. His hands were hidden in the opposite sleeve, and his head was recessed to the back of his hood. He was taller than average, about eight and half hands if Marcus were to guess. He was thin on the risk of gauntness, giving his cheeks a sallow appearance, made worse by a jutting chin and a nose that seemed too long for the rest of his face. His eyes were dark and foreboding. All in all, Sinifir looked as sinister as Marcus knew him to be.

"Friends and fellow servants of the King."

Marcus could already feel the mind-touch. Sinifir was reaching out to everyone present, convincing them to relax and accept everything he was about to say. It nauseated Marcus to see that he was succeeding.

A sudden thought came to his mind. *If Sinifir could mind-cast, perhaps he could do the same.* Marcus conjured up the image of a large, venomous snake, wrapped in a hooded black robe. Its face was in the image of Sinifir's. He cast this image to everyone assembled, save Sinifir and Captain Morris, superimposing it in parallel to the other. A look of shock and disbelief passed over the combatants' bowed heads. *A talking snake?* The message could not have been more clear. Among the more irreverent, there was an undercurrent of humor. The remainder kept absolute silence in shock and fear. Whether he realized it or not, Sinifir's day had become tainted . Marcus struggled to keep a hidden smile from his lips. Ivan, Greta and Thomas, knowing exactly who was responsible and what was afoot, had the same difficulty. Marcus could only hope this sinister image would remain in the mind of each combatant.

At last, Sinifir finished his platitudes to the King, to Captain Morris, and to the combatants. At the direction of Captain Morris, the combatants assembled in an arc and faced a target some three paces away. At the designated signal, each drew a dagger and cast it into the target. Ivan's blade arrived a fraction of a second before Marcus'. But the latter struck the target's heart. Other daggers quickly followed. Two blades, arriving at about the same time, interfered with each other, failed to penetrate, then fell to the ground. Captain Morris cringed in embarrassment. Sinifir showed no emotion. But Marcus had no doubt he had taken note of those who had succeeded, and who had not.

The second event, bolt-casting, had a similar result, but without the embarrassment of a failure. The heavier bolts penetrated through any potential interference and embedded firmly in the distant target, about a five-pace distant. With his *gift*-enhanced speed, Marcus was the first to draw and load, but then hesitated, allowing half of the others to cast. When he did so, his bolt again found the target's heart. *A competent demonstration. But not one to draw more attention to myself.*

Sinifir seemed pleased with the result. One of the last to cast, unfortunately, was one whose blade had fallen to the ground. Eljay. Marcus' one thought was *now we are down to a hand and one.*

"Captain Morris, I should like to meet your trainees individually. Please introduce them to me. I want them to tell me a bit about themselves, their background and profession."

Captain Morris was quick to comply. He began calling trainees up one-by-one. Marcus used a light mind-touch to intercept whatever Sinifir tried to impress on each trainee. The dark mage was deviously clever. As each trainee revealed his name and profession, Sinifir would divine a weakness and attempt to exploit it.

Camden was the first to approach. "Camden, m'Lord. I'm from the village of Klem, but now live here in the capitol. I am a ..." he shrugged, "... a thief, m'Lord."

Sinifir snorted. "An honest man. That I can admire."

Marcus could feel Camden's mind fill with images of wealth, gold and silver in abundance. Camden took a sudden breath. "M'Lord." Any lingering memory of a talking snake was forgotten. Camden was now Sinifir's, purchased by greed and paid in promises. Marcus wanted to be ill.

And so it went. Sinifir had an uncanny ability to entice. He used wealth, power, passion. He always found a weakness to exploit. To his great relief, as he mind-touched Ivan, Greta and Thomas, he sensed only a brick or stone wall. They would leave the interview with no influence imposed upon them by Sinifir.

It finally came down to Marcus, the last. "You are particularly adept with weapons, young man. Your name?"

"Marcus, m'Lord. Blades-man trainee in the military."

"You are very good, for being a mere trainee. Why do you think that is so?"

"Unknown, m"Lord. Blessed with good reflexes and a good eye, perhaps?"

"Yes, perhaps, as you say. And you hesitated in firing your cross-bow?"

Marcus was surprised Sinifir has observed that slight delay. "Yes, m'Lord. I wanted to be sure of my aim. There were many bolts flying to the target at the same time." Again, Marcus wasn't sure if Sinifir believed him. He could have closed his mind with that, but was curious how Sinifir perceived him and his weaknesses. Images of standing at the front of ranks and ranks of soldiers filled his mind. It was a promise of power over others. Marcus smiled inwardly, knowing it was all a lie. Sinifir had perceived him incorrectly. *He had, right?* Marcus turned, head still bowed, and withdrew from the front of the dais.

Captain Morris had dismissed everyone after the review, explaining the training was over until directed otherwise by Sinifir. Marcus said his farewell to friends Ivan, Greta and Thomas. They thought his superimposition of a snake's image over Sinifir's opening remarks was brilliant. Ivan had said "I don't remember a thing Sinifir told us, but I will never forget that talking snake. Seemed to be a precise fit, at least, in my mind it was." Greta and Thomas had agreed with a nod. Marcus told them what they had missed during the interview.

"Sinifir was much, much more devious that I expected. He has completely entranced three, maybe four of our group. It will be interesting to see how many make it to the next round."

"You think there will be another round?" asked Ivan.

"'Course there will be," said Thomas.

"For sure," said Greta. "We haven't gotten to the poisons yet, like Marcus told us days ago. That will be just after swearing an oath of total secrecy and loyalty to the King, to him, and to each other. By the way, that oath of silence and mutual support? Same thing happens in the thieves' guild. They swear on their lives not to betray each other. These are always a work of dark secret and evil deed. I'm sure Sinifir will make us do the same."

They agreed on a method to reach one another should the need arise.

CHAPTER
NINE

The following first-day found Marcus back in his previous assignment with his trainee blades-men. It was hard to think of them as trainees, though. They had progressed very well under blade-master Kelson's tutelage. He had passed them on position and forms, and had begun training them on strategy and style. Nevertheless, Marcus had them all return to practicing fundamentals. They were not going to strategy and style until *he* was satisfied. He watched them carefully. They were good, it was sure. But not yet perfect.

As always, it began with *tai kai*. They had all learned the four-hands-two fundamental moves. Marcus went through the motions with them, watching carefully. Each move was a carefully orchestrated blade-fighting move, either for offense or defense. Satisfied, he had them repeat the steps, flowing gracefully from one to another, but with greater speed. Then again, always faster. Katrina was the only one who could maintain perfect form in the end. With *real* long blades, and at the highest of speeds, *tai kai* between two facing blades-men was referred to as *blade dancing*. It could be performed with one blade or two. Marcus had Katrina come forward. While the class watched, they faced each other and together went through all four-hand-two moves as quickly as she could manage. Each held two wooden blades. They ended to the hoots and cheers of the others.

Katrina whispered to him as she left for the day. *"Tonight. Same time and place as before."*

He nodded in reply.

Marcus had no difficulty slipping away in the late evening. He arrived at the normal rendezvous. But Katrina was not there. It grew darker. He began wondering if she would show at all, when she suddenly emerged from the dense shrubbery surrounding the palms. "I don't have much time. Stephen saw me leave, or I think he did. Not that he suspects me in particular. He just suspects everything, and everyone."

Marcus nodded in understanding.

"I've missed you, while you were away."

"Is Kelson not training you well?"

Katrina blushed. "Not talking about training."

"Oh." Now it was Marcus' turn to blush.

Katrina: "Too bad we're cousins. It breaks my heart."

Marcus: "Second cousins." A few moments of silence passed. "Any feedback on our training?"

Katrina brought her focus back to the reason they were meeting. "Oh, for certain. But first you need to know how the more important things are going. It is not good for Sinifir and Stephen. They are both furious."

"There's good news, then?"

"Yes and no. Good for us, bad for my father and your grandfather. My father is crown prince, as you know, so my grandfather the King has to listen to him. Your grandfather, 'that meddling fool' as Sinifir calls him, has taken my father into his confidence. And convinced him of Sinifir's true nature, a dark mage. My father has *gift*, limited in power, but it has made him somewhat immune to Sinifir's influences now that he knows what to expect. Unfortunately, Sinifir still prevails with my grandfather, who as far as I can tell, has very little *gift*. So they – my father and your grandfather -- have decided on an 'if you can't beat them, join them' strategy. It has been working brilliantly. First they convinced my grandfather that a royal should lead the army against Caldonia. So now my father controls the army and is responsible for its war preparations. He immediately explained the situation to all the generals. Forewarned, forearmed. Sinifir will now have to remove my father and all the senior military leaders if he wants to take on Caldonia. And what's even more devastating to Sinifir, my father has opened direct negotiations with Caldonia. In the spirit of 'reconciliation and peace'."

"No wonder Sinifir is furious. This really makes it difficult..."

"...not so fast, Marcus. This is where your group of assassins comes into play."

"They wouldn't take out your father, the generals..."

"... and your grandfather? Sinifir has no regard whatsoever for the lives of others, only for his blind ambition. And Stephen shares his vision and lust for power."

"Well, there are no assassins, yet. What was Sinifir's reaction to our review last seven-day?"

"Well, he and Stephen had a lot to discuss. Sinifir has an incredible memory, I'll give him that much. He was able to recall the name and performance of every trainee. Good news. He has reduced the list to eight. Better news. You're not one of them. It appears he has the ability to detect *gift* in others. So, understandably, he had some concerns about you."

"I can guess who the eight are: My three friends, plus Louton, Lindon, Carlos, Matthew and..." He paused, thinking. "Camden. How did I do?"

"Looks like you and Sinifir think alike," she said somewhat sarcastically.

"I've lived and fought with them for a full turning. It only took Sinifir a matter of moments. He is a truly frightening mind-mage."

"Well, this is where things lie for now. Sinifir wants to continue assassin training soon, very soon. Probably within a seven-day or two. I'll keep you advised. Now, it's time for me to get back. Bye." She surprised Marcos by grabbing him and giving him a peck on the cheek. "Just too bad we're cousins."

"Second cousins," said Marcus.

"Yes, but cousins nonetheless." With that and a final sigh, she slipped back into the shrubbery and was gone.

Marcus stood before his assembled cadre of trainees. "You have all been wondering why I took you back to practicing fundamentals. Let me explain. In a real fight, with real blades, there's offense and defense. You will have to master both to survive. The fundament steps and movements you have learned and practiced in *tai kai* will protect you against most offensive moves. But only if you can react quickly enough. Let me say it differently. Fundamentals keep you alive long enough to employ whatever strategy you want to use in offense. But fundamentals have to be learned so well as to be automatic, almost reflexive. And absolutely precise. The good news is that I think you are now at that point and ready to move on. We will begin offensive training on those parts of *tai kai* that take advantage of an opponent's weaknesses."

The trainees had different levels of natural ability. But all were focused and worked hard to duplicate the moves they were shown. The day passed quickly. Again, the most able student was Katrina. He did a gentle mind-touch and found... *gift?* He was sure of it. Strange that he had not noticed it before. But then, he had had no particular reason to look for it. And they had been apart for a full turning.

Saul and Marcus had dined together. The meal was finished and cleared away. As if some unspoken signal had been given, they simultaneously began to speak. Marcus raised his hands. "You first, grandfather. But I might already know some of what you want to tell me."

" I would be surprised if you did. So, what have you heard?"

"Let's see. Jared, the Crown Prince, is now in charge of the army, much to Sinifir's annoyance. And he has requested an envoy from Caldonia to 'negotiate peace' or some other such nonsense. I say *nonsense* because we're not in any conflict except one of Sinifir's creation. Those, I guess, are the high points."

"I don't know your source of information, but it's pretty good. I could fill in few details, but you have the essence of it. What news do you have to share?"

"Assassin training, at the least the initial phase, has ended. I'm back to training new blades-men. I'm sure Sinifir will be narrowing down the class to the few he thinks have the requisite skills. And over whom he has sufficient control. Fortunately, I'm not going to be on his list. Despite my precautions, Sinifir has detected my *gift* and suspects he will have little influence on my mind. But I have three friends that have been accepted. I've taken them into my confidence and I believe they can be trusted. They know I'm a mage, but not my relationship to you. And they understand Sinifir's nature and intent. I've told them what to look for when Sinifir tries to influence them, and how to resist. I hope it will be enough. But grandfather, Sinifir's power is formidable. And he is totally without conscience, as you know. I'm expecting him to move in the next several seven-days to swear them into some kind of secret cabal. And thereafter initiate another round of training. He will probably start them on killing strokes, poisons, and other things similar."

Saul's face fell at the news. "Sadly, it is much as we feared. Actually it is worse, moving at a more rapid pace than we dared hope. I say *we* hoped, as I include the Crown Prince in these concerns. You know we have also enlisted our generals in this conflict?"

"Yes, I know. When Sinifir moves to seize the kingdom, he will need to assassinate a large number of people. And pretty much all at the same time. That would include the King, Crown Prince Jared, the generals. And you. Well, he might spare the King. If they should succeed, I believe the King's remaining life would be brief. Prince Stephen is anxious to assume the throne"

Saul thought for a moment. "There is one more dimension to this, something that might give Sinifir reason to wait. Not forever, of course, but perhaps for a few seven-days, maybe more."

"And that would be?"

"The envoy from Caldonia you mentioned. We have asked them to send a negotiator to us here, in Iber. Crossing the Betting Sea is no small feat. We think it would be several seven-days before the meeting could take place. Sinifir will want to wait for that meeting to take place. The conference would be an ideal opportunity to initiate hostilities with Caldonia. Perhaps by assassinating the Caldonian envoy? Or more likely, he would assassinate someone here and then place blame on Caldonia for the deed. Do you think your assassin team will be ready in less than three seven-days?"

"*My* assassin team? You're not serious, no? And to answer your question, unfortunately, yes I do. Three or four of the ones I trained with are by their very nature, assassins already. They will not hesitate to kill for coin."

"Your team? Slip of my tongue. Please forgive me. I will pass your assessment on to Crown Prince Jared. In the meantime, there's something that you and I must address. This seven-day. I've talked to Kelson and he has agreed to cover your class, third-day through sixth. You will need to dismiss training tomorrow mid-day and meet me here. We need to do some shopping. Oh, and retrieve a cross-bow from the armory and a quiver of bolts."

CHAPTER

TEN

It was second-day. Marcus had followed his grandfather's instructions and dismissed the class at mid-day, with nary a complaint from the students. He and his grandfather had arrived home at nearly the same time. Saul retrieved his coin purse from its not-so-hidden hiding place and signaled for Marcus to follow. They left the castle through its west gate, an archway that opened up into Alexa's main market.

Despite being a life-long resident of the capitol, Marcus had spent but little time outside the castle itself. He and his grandfather were well attended and fed in the royal suites. And he had possessed little interest in the affairs and events beyond the castle walls. Saul led the way to a merchant specializing in outdoor clothing and traveling supplies.

A salesman, seeing the two well-dressed men, was quick to offer his assistance. "Gentlemen, how may I help you this fine day?"

Saul responded. "We, my companion and I, must undertake a three-day trip beyond the castle walls, beyond Claron Falls. We will need appropriate clothing, as well as camping equipment for the duration. I trust you can accommodate us?"

"Most assuredly. But sir, there are no roads beyond the Falls. It is just a dark, damp, forested wilderness, quite full of dangerous beasts. You are sure of your direction?"

"Quite."

"I see. Well, let's begin with clothing. You will want hooded seal-skin capes. seal skin over-breeches, wool stockings and high leather boots. They will be a bit warm but will keep you dry." He went on to name other articles of clothing. He had obviously done this many times before, as he was thorough and quick. "As to non-clothing requirements, how are you planning to eat? Will you be carrying provisions or will you be living off the land? If the latter, you will need a cooking pot, a few basic utensils for preparing and eating your food, and a few staples such as salt and fat. And you will also need a ground-cloth and tent. I would not advise sleeping without some form of protection, both below and above."

The negotiations went on for some time. The clothing was put to one side, provisions to the other. "I trust we can come and pick up the provisions as we depart in the morning?"

"Of course, sir. Would that be early?"

"Yes, shortly after first light. If that can be arranged."

"We will arrange it into two packs. And with suitable carrying straps, if you wish."

"Yes, please."

Marcus saw the merchant add carrying straps to the account.

"Now, how do you wish to settle the bill?"

Saul placed his coin purse on the counter. "And how much do we owe?"

The merchant took a few moments to tally the list. "It comes to two and sixteen."

Marcus had no idea if two silvers and sixteen coppers were a fair price, but he did a light mind-touch and found, to his relief, the man was honest. Saul picked through his coin purse and retrieved three silvers.

"Thank you for your services. You may keep the balance for yourself and those who will be preparing the packs for us." It was a four-copper add, and the merchant looked pleased. "Until tomorrow, then" said Saul, and he and Marcus took their leave, bearing the packaged clothing in their arms.

Dawn came and Marcus dressed quickly. The merchant had had a good eye for size, as his clothing fit well. The seal-skin was a bit stiff, to be expected for new fabric, but Marcus was sure it would become supple soon enough. They took an early, hearty breakfast, and retrieved a small bag of provisions from the castle kitchens. Saul gave the bag to Marcus to carry. He took a quick peek inside: a block of cheese, a sausage, two loaves of bread, and two leather flagons of water. Probably a day's worth of food. Marcus wondered if his grandfather had plans for days two and three. If not, he was ably prepared to forage for their food, and cook it as well.

They left the castle and arrived without incident at the outfitter's store. At that early time, and it being a third-day, the streets were mostly empty. The same salesman that served them the previous day was waiting, two packs at his feet. One was quite a bit larger than the other. Marcus had no doubt which would be his. They shouldered their respective loads and walked briskly to the west, in the direction of Claron Falls and the wilderness beyond.

The Kingdom of Iber fully encompassed the Island of the same name. It lay west of the mainland, with the treacherous Betting Sea separating the two. Its long eastern shoreline, facing the mainland, was composed of shear cliffs. The island interior had a temperate climate in the south, stretching to an alpine, sub-arctic environment in the far north, then passing to an even harsher clime. The inland areas had many small holdings of fertility, but were mostly composed of rocky meadows. Second- and third-turning run-off from the mountains to the north and west fed a myriad of streams and small rivers. Forests abounded, and within them a plentiful supply of deer and other game animals. Together, the island provided ample food for a stable population, but not for an increasing one. It had a diversity of minerals as well. Their abundance made mining and smithing locally profitable, but for export, not. There was plentiful gold of high quality in the Isor mountains, but it was difficult to recover.

Iber's vast eastern coastline provided but two ports, Nordsport and Sudsport, the latter being much the larger of the two. Both were navigable throughout the turn, except on exceptionally cold fourth and first turnings when Nordsport became ice-bound. Both ports hosted a small but important fishing fleet. And there was a modest merchant fleet that challenged the Betting Sea to exchange Iber's goods with those from the mainland. Mostly, it was wood products for luxury items, exotic foods, and wrought metal. Taken as a whole, Iber was a large, self-sustaining island that had existed in peaceful isolation and independence for over one hand two fist turns.

Alexa, the capitol and largest city of the Kingdom, was situated in the southern-most area of the island. It lay close against the Claron mountain range to its west, in a pocket of relatively fertile land. It was three-fist leagues east to reach Sudsport over a well-traveled and passable road. Nordsport was more than three-fist leagues farther, north and east. There was a road, not much more than a path really, connecting to Alexa. It passed over the massive Isor mountains, over countless rivers, and through many rocky rills and canyons. It was rarely traveled in the second and third turnings, closed in fourth and first. Goods to and from Nordsport invariably went by ship, not by land. Nordsport primarily supported the scattered villages and towns on the north- and north-central highlands of the island.

By noon Saul and Marcus had ascended the foothills leading to the Claron Falls. Along the way they passed scattered homesteads where hearty Iberians managed small herds of sheep and goats. They encountered logging camps as they gained elevation. It was shortly after mid-day when they reached Claron Falls itself. The waterfall was a spectacular display of nature, and a small town -- village to be more accurate -- had arisen to support the few tourists determined enough to make a day's hike to experience the sight. Saul and Marcus paused for a brief respite and purchased a late mid-day meal from the only inn in the village. The marked path ended at the inn.

Saul surprised his grandson by being a reasonably competent woodsman. He directed them along subtle game trails, pointing out edible plants, berries and tubers along the way. Marcus, of course, knew these plants as well, but kept silent. Darkness descended quickly after the sun dipped below the tree-line. It was the time of a new moon. In the dying light, Marcus pointed to a small clearing in the forest. "Let's set up camp there." They went to work and soon the tent, ground-cloths and bedding were in place. Marcus went about collecting fallen branches for a flame while his grandfather spread out the remainder of their provisions.

"Tomorrow, you will need to hunt for food. We will be stopping at mid-day and going no farther." Marcus cast a flame to ignite the wood and the two of them settled down to eat their cold meal. The bread was still crisp, the cheese fresh, the sausage good. Marcus could have eaten more, but made no mention of it to his grandfather. With the flame properly banked for the night, they undressed and retired to their bedrolls.

Until now, Marcus had been content to simply follow his grandfather's direction. It would have been disrespectful to question, argue or refuse. But after a long, arduous day of travel, his curiosity got the best of him. "Grandfather, I'm sure you have a purpose for this camping adventure, but the reason escapes me entirely. Am I out of line to ask why?"

Saul did not immediately reply. "Tomorrow, my son. It will all be made clear tomorrow." With that he turned his back to Marcus and went to sleep. Normally, Marcus would have lain awake pondering their situation, but weariness overtook him and he, too, was soon asleep.

It was a clear, crisp morning. The sun was up, but given the deep forest surrounding them, it would not be visible for some time to come. They arose, dressed, and refolded the tent and bedding. Marcus went to stir the coals and rekindle the flame from the night before. Saul gave a grunt followed by a terse command. "I will be foraging some greens for our breakfast. Go and find us fresh meat."

Marcus left camp. He knew there was a spring of fresh water about a fist of paces down-hill, as they had filled the water flagons there the night before. As he approached the natural watering hole, he extended *gift* to sense life-force. He detected some form of animal or animals, though he couldn't tell what kind or how many. He stealthily approached, parted the foliage, and saw wild pigs drinking from the spring. A *hofa* and three piglets. He drew his cross-bow, loaded a bolt, and took careful aim at one of the piglets. Without hesitation, he used *gift* to guide the bolt exactly to its target, the neck of the largest piglet. It dropped to the ground without a sound. The sow and the remaining two piglets fled with squeals of fright. Marcus retrieved and cleaned the bolt, lifted the piglet to his shoulders, and returned to camp.

Saul sat by the flame, stirring a pot of boiling water. There was some kind of vegetable in the pot that Marcus did not recognize. "Well done, my son. Now clean it for cooking."

This was not something he had seen done in siege training. "Uh, I don't know how. Could you show..."

Saul cut him off with a chuckle. "Bring it here, and I'll show you how it's done." Taking a few swift strokes with his short-blade, he bled the pig, sliced open its abdomen, and removed the entrails. He then proceeded to skin the carcass, tossing the entrails and hide into the bushes. "There will be feasting for the scavengers by night-fall, I think. Now go, get me a couple of green twigs to make a spit. One with a fork in it."

Marcus did what he was told and soon the piglet was roasting over the flame, It wasn't a large animal, but certainly enough for several meals. "It looks like we have enough for lunch, too. You chose well, Marcus."

The flame burned down to a bed or red-hot coals and the piglet cooked quickly. It had a hard, dark crust that tasted very good. Along with the cooked vegetable (which his grandfather never identified by name), it was a very satisfying start to the day. Marcus carefully extinguished the flame, as had been taught during siege training, and erased the obvious traces of their campsite. It was probably not needed, but was standard practice in the military. It wouldn't fool an experienced tracker, of course. But his grandfather pronounced it 'good enough'. Saul wrapped the left-over piglet in some large leaves he had gathered from the forest. They shouldered their packs and were soon on their way again.

Beginning about mid-day, Saul began looking for a campsite. Each time they came across a clearing or meadow, he would stop and look about, always muttering something like, 'Nope, not yet' or 'not here'. Marcus had no idea what his grandfather was looking for and could do nothing but nod, and move on. They stopped for a lunch of cold piglet, managing to eat it all. A short time later they burst from the woods into a wide, open field, approximately rectangular, about five-hand paces on a side. "Yes! Perfect! This is just what we need!" Saul went to the middle of the field and shed his pack with a welcome sigh. The field was relatively flat, with a small stream trickling down one side close to the tree line. At his grandfather's command, Marcus went in search of more game. "Look for something larger, if you can, Marcus. Enough for today and tomorrow as well."

It took Marcus some time to find, stalk and slay a small deer. He placed it over his shoulders and made his way back to camp. Saul told him to dress it for cooking. "Just follow the same steps I showed you for the piglet." Marcus did his best. It wasn't very neat, especially the skinning part. But his grandfather seemed satisfied and instructed him to gather wood for cooking their food.

"And we will need rocks to build a flame pit," Saul shouted after him.

A short time later Marcus had retrieved a hand and two rocks, about two-hands in diameter, and dumped them near the place his grandfather had pitched the tents. He had also pulled together a sizeable pile of dry branches. They were plentiful in the forest surrounding the glade. Again, his grandfather had foraged for plant edibles. He had found a sizeable quantity of bulbs, stems and flowers still attached. These Marcus recognized, but again, left his grandfather to boast of his success. Saul pointed to the tubers. "I think you will like these a bit better than the pie plants we had last night. Pie plants are edible, but these... much better!"

Saul quartered the deer, wrapping three of the pieces in leaves, as he had done the left-over piglet. Without being asked, Marcus had found green branches and fashioned a spit over the burn-pit. Once the flame had burned down, a deer hind-quarter was placed on the spit and the bulbs placed in the pot. The coals were hot, the water boiled, and the deer cooked quickly. Saul turned the spit often to make sure the venison was thoroughly and evenly done. At last, they sat down cross-legged before the dying coals to enjoy their meal. Marcus took the pot and their plates to the stream for cleaning. When he returned, his grandfather pointed to the ground next to him. "Sit. Now we talk."

"Marcus, what do you remember about your recent bout of *gift-sickness*?"

"Well, I remember feeling really good, then suddenly I wasn't. The next thing I recall, I was in the hospital infirmary."

"Yes. And do you remember what I said about *gift* and new moons?"

"You said that *gift* flowed in a great river around the earth. And that it was strongest when the sun and moon pulled on the earth together. As in now, during a new moon. And it is weakest with a full moon, when they pull in opposite directions."

"Exactly. I'm glad you paid attention. Now, how long between consecutive new moons?"

"I don't know exactly. Three-hand days? That's how long a lunar cycle is, right?"

"You are close, but not exact. Actually, it is almost exactly two-hand nine and a half days. Do you remember what time of the day you suffered *gift-sickness*?"

"Well, it was after mid-day, a short while after our mid-day meal for sure."

"Correct! So today, being the two-hand nine days hence, we should have the next new moon sometime tonight. Would you agree?"

"Yes, if what you say is true. And I believe that to be so."

"So tonight, we lie awake waiting for the new moon to align again, for the surge to occur. And when it does, you must be in contact with the ground and pull *gift* to you once again."

"And suffer *gift-sickness*, as I did before?"

"No, Marcus, I will be here to prevent that from happening. But if you are able to pull *gift* to yourself, well, it's important I know that you are able."

"But why here, out in the middle of the Claron Mountains? Couldn't we do it there, in Alexa, just as well?"

"One thing at a time, Marcus. One thing at a time. First, let's see if you can draw *gift* to yourself. We will lie down together, and you will tell me what you are feeling."

Saul had Marcus remove his shoes and wool stockings and recline on the warm ground next to the banked flame. As Saul had explained, it was important for Marcus to actually be in contact with the earth. As the time passed, they kept up a running dialogue about the nature of *gift*.

"Have you ever seen maps of our known world, Marcus?"

"Yes, of course. I've seen them many times, in my early schooling."

"Have you ever noticed that the major cities, the kingdom capitols, lie in a straight line east-to-west?"

"They do? No, I never noticed that at all."

"They do. You can draw a straight line from Alexa to the capitols of Caldonia, Suerca, Tumano and Adnium. And that line passes through some of the other great cities of the mainland, as well. And now you are supposed to ask why this is important."

"Why is that important?"

"I told you *gift* flowed in a great river around the earth, right?"

"Yes."

"The line between the great cities, that's the path the river of *gift* takes. It passes through, or actually under, all of these great cities. Now, you are supposed to ask why that is so important. Go ahead, ask."

"Why is that important?"

"Because it gave the powerful mages of old great access to *gift*. They could readily draw from it during new moons. And what else do all these great cities have, that sets them apart from all others?"

Marcus shrugged. "Greater population? More wealth?"

"Close. They all have stone castles. Great *old* stone castles. Castles that go back many, many hand-fists, well beyond our recorded history. You've seen pictures?"

"Engravings in some of the school manuscripts? Yes, they all had great foundations and walls."

"Have you ever wondered how the foundations and wall-stones of those castle were quarried and put into place? How they are smooth and perfectly fitted together? I tell you how. Anciently, there were mages with great endowments of *earth-gift*. Working together they could call forth great stones from deep within the earth and manipulate them into shape and position. But to do that, they had to be close, very close, to a source of *gift*. Our castle foundations in Alexa are more modest. Because by the time our castle was built, much of that ancient power had been lost. Or if not lost, greatly diminished."

"Which is why the cities lie on the top of the great river of *gift*?"

"Precisely. And above reservoirs of great stone. That's why Iber lies so far from the Betting Sea. And why so many of the mainland capitols are in odd places. So, why are we here, immediately west of Alexa? Because we have followed the great river of *gift* farther west. It flows exactly beneath us."

""But why here, so distant from Alexa?"

"That is another discussion. First, let's see if you can draw upon *gift* as you did a moon-cycle ago."

More time passed, mid-night came and went. Marcus broke the silence. "I'm beginning to feel the pull of *gift*."

"How does it affect you?"

"I feel well. Strong. Energetic. Healthy. Is it just more life-force I'm feeling?"

"Yes. Now, reach out with your mind and embrace it, invite it to come to you. Pull it to you. Can you do that?"

"It's what I was doing. It's what I am doing. Oh. Grandfather, here it comes, the same surge as before!"

Saul jumped to his feet and put his hands under Marcus' armpits. "Let me know as soon as you want it to stop. But allow as much as you can tolerate to flow into you."

Marcus nodded. "I'm... I'm feeling well for now, but it's

building rapidly." A brief moment passed. "No more, no more. Make it stop!"

With surprising strength, Saul lifted Marcus from the ground. The distress on Marcus' face withdrew. "How do you feel, son?"

"I'm not hurting anywhere, if that's what you mean. But I feel like I'm – I don't know how to describe it – that my skin is about to burst."

Saul had also felt the surge of *gift*, though for him it was a slight tingling in his feet. It passed, and he laid Marcus back on the ground. "I want you to cast flame, ignite our stack of wood. But be very careful. I fear you *gift-power* is greatly enhanced right now."

Marcus did as instructed, projecting a minuscule amount of *gift* while mentally invoking flame's word of power, *fo-see-AH*. The bundle of branches exploded, scattering burning sticks in all directions. Both men stared in disbelief.

"Dangerous," said Saul.

Marcus nodded. "Most certainly. Now what?"

"You need to send some of the *gift* back from whence it came. Focus on the ground. Cast *gift* into the earth."

Marcus placed his hands on the soil at his feet, and cast *gift* into the soil. He could feel the power of *gift* pass through both his hands and feet. "It's working. But do I need to be touching the ground to make it work?"

"That I don't know. Here, stand on our packs and see what you can do."

Marcus did so, the flow of *gift-power* continued. "It works either way. I'm going to quit casting, if I can." In his mind, Marcus withdrew the command to cast *gift*, and the process stopped. "So it seems I need to be contact *with* the earth to pull *gift*, but not to return it?"

"So it appears. Perhaps, when you have greater experience in pulling *gift*, that might change. But that's enough for tonight. We will do more testing in the morning."

They retired to their bedrolls. It was quite some time before either could drift off to sleep.

Marcus awoke before Saul, dressed, and went about gathering more flame-wood. By the time he returned with his third bundle of branches, Saul was awake and dressed. "Quite a night, wouldn't you say?"

"Yes, quite a night! Now what? Hopefully breakfast, I'm totally famished."

They soon had a deer quarter over the coals with bulbs again boiling in the pot. It was the same meal as the night before, but neither complained. Marcus took the cookware and eating utensils to the stream and cleaned them.

Saul: "Questions?"

Marcus: "Yes, a few."

Saul: "I want you to try some things, before you ask them. See that tree, standing alone on the edge of the field?"

Marcus pointed to the tree he thought his grandfather had selected. "That one, with the yellow flowers at its base?"

"Yes, that's the one. Reach out with *gift*. Tell me if you can sense its life-force."

Marcus did as his grandfather asked. "Yes, I can feel its life-force. There isn't much, but it's there."

"Now I want you to *pull* its life-force to you, much like you reached for *gift* last night."

Marcus pulled, the life force came. He felt a small stimulus to his body, not unlike the reaction of a morning cup of *kuff*. The tree seemed to quiver and wilt before their eyes, its limbs taking on a marked droop. Saul looked on sadly and began to weep. Between sobs, he managed to blurt out "and this is why we are deep in the forest!"

Saul's crying slowed to an end. Eventually he gained some

control of his emotions, but remained silent and pensive. Marcus also sat quietly, respecting his grandfather's silence.

With a sigh, Saul began to explain. "Marcus, what kind of mage is the most dangerous of all? And why? Or asked a different way, which endowment of *gift* is most to be feared?"

Marcus shrugged his shoulders. "The most frightening one I know of, is a dark mage like Sinifir. He is a mind-mage. So I would think his type would be the most dangerous."

"Why? What makes him the most dangerous?"

"Because he can influence others? And the inclination to use his endowment in an evil manner in doing so?"

"An excellent reply. But most certainly incorrect."

Marcus waited for his grandfather to say more.

"To understand the *correct* answer, we need to go back into history, the history of Iber itself, to the first Marcus Aurelius. He is, was, your namesake, and unquestionably the greatest mage of his day. Perhaps the strongest mage of whom we have any record. There were undoubtedly stronger, but of those we have only myth. Marcus the First was a good man from what I understand. Nevertheless, he brought about the downfall of his King and the destruction of his kingdom. Well, perhaps destruction is a strong word. Marcus the First *was* destroyed, the king and his people were banished from the mainland and driven to this island. They were told never to return. That was over one-hand two fist turns ago. "

Marcus: "So what was so dangerous about Marcus the First that brought about such a calamity?"

"He was..." Saul stopped and began weeping once again. Finally he was able to continue. "He was a *master* mage, a mage capable of absorbing the *gift* and *power* of any other mage. When this became known, the mages of Tumano grew fearful and tried to *silence* him. But he single-handedly destroyed *them,* by absorbing their mage-power and turning it against them. So Tumano came with an army." Saul had begun to cry again. "He destroyed many, casting them deep into the earth. There was peace for several turns, for Marcus and his king were not ambitious for wealth or power. But the fear of Marcus spread to all four mainland kingdoms. They amassed their mages, over five fists strong, along with a great combined army. All with the intent of destroying him. At the direction of his King, Marcus was prepared to go against them all. And would probably have prevailed. But when the armies fell upon the citizens of the Kingdom and began to slay *them*, Marcus surrendered himself to make the slaughter end. They killed him in a cruel manner to which he gave no resistance. In fear of another master mage arising with like power, the capitol city was destroyed. And the kingdom in its entirely was banished to this isle, becoming thereafter the Kingdom of Iber. And as a further condition, King Justin was forced to issue an everlasting decree: that any master mage that should arise in the future, from the Aurelius line, was to be put to death before he or she should develop and exert that level of power again. The name Marcus *Aureleus* is long forgotten, but throughout the known world, the decree to destroy any new *master mage* that arises still stands. Notwithstanding, that first king of Iber vowed that the name Marcus Aurelius would forever be held in memory and respect among his people."

"That is why you told me the 'big dog' story turns ago. And now that you know what I am, or could become, you are obliged to put me to death?" said Marcus, sadly.

"The story I told you has passed from generation to generation. And the oath? I swore it upon becoming a high-mage. It is the same oath my father, and his fathers before him took, before they assumed the office I now hold."

"And I am to simply look on, while you execute the terms and conditions of your office? Are you planning to do it here, now, without witnesses? What if I choose to resist? Do you think you can overpower me? I think not, not now. You should have executed your obligations to the oath before I emerged, or soon after. Just when did you suspect I had emerged as a master mage?"

"You were dark-born, as was the first Marcus Aurelius. I don't believe anyone has understood what that really meant. You were born at the pinnacle of a lunar passing, the moon and sun perfectly aligned, when *gift power* would have been at its absolute strongest. I suspect that is what has always been meant by being *dark born*. There might be more written in the early *Kult* record of the Chronicles. But in the past two-hand five pages, written in *Turga*, it has only been mentioned once. And it applied specifically to Marcus the First."

Marcus remembered reading it in one of the oldest records he could read. It had meant nothing to him when he had copied it to the new parchment.

"Your parents were strong in *gift*, and you were born directly over the *gift-river* flowing beneath the castle. There could not have been more portentous conditions. Your early emergence and maturity were also harbingers of greatness. But it wasn't until you said you could cast *gift* to control your weapons that my suspicions were fully aroused. Your bout with *gift* sickness was another confirmation. But I was still in denial. Here, now, I no longer am. You are, or will become, a *master mage*. And there is nothing I can do to prevent it. We both know that even now you are much stronger than I am. And you grow stronger from cycle to cycle. Not only do I lack the power to destroy you, but I would not, could not, ever do so. My oath notwithstanding."

"And that is because?' asked Marcus.

"First and foremost..." Saul blinked a tear from his eyes, "I could never destroy the son I love. You are a son to me, and always will be. A second reason is that with Sinifir, you are probably the only person strong enough to keep Iber from falling into his grasp. All I can hope for is that you will be able, throughout your life, to keep your power sufficiently hidden to escape the death sentence that perpetually hangs over your head. And that, as a master mage, known or not, you will be able to constrain your power. That you will not destroy those who will surely combine to contend against you. Marcus, if you were to become a dark mage, no one would have power to stand against you. It was this fear that brought an end to Marcus the First, his king, *and* his kingdom."

Marcus gave the entire conversation a careful thought. "Then grandfather, let's agree to one thing. You and I will take no action against each other until our common enemy, Sinifir, has been eliminated. We will deal with the rest of this in its aftermath."

"So agreed, my son. You now understand why we have come to such a remote location? We had to go to a place no one could possibly observe. Our work here is nearly finished. There is one more matter of testing I think we should resolve."

"And that is?"

"It's possible a mage such as yourself has access *all gift* endowments. Which is why he is referred to as a *master* mage. I know you already have many. You have demonstrated *gift* in battle, healing and mind-touch. But you should know where your true strength lies. Marcus the First was profoundly strong in *earth-gift*. And it served him well. I would see if the same holds true with you."

"And how would you test for *earth-gift*?"

"As we tested for flame, turnings ago, I will teach you a word of power and you will demonstrate your strength in its use. The word is *tier*."

"*Tier*? That's it?"

"*Tier*, yes, but you must pronounce it correctly: tee-AIR. It is a powerful word when coupled with strong *gift*. I want you to imagine a hole in the ground, or rather a depression, say a pace long, five hands wide, and eight hands deep. When you have it clearly in your mind, cast *gift* while invoking the word *tier*."

Marcus did as directed. He felt a small out-rush of power as the soil sank into the precise dimensions he had imagined. He had a sudden, foreboding thought: the depression was the dimensions of a grave.

"As I thought. I suppose now there is little reason for us to linger in this dark and depressing forest."

The trip back to Alexa was quiet and uneventful/ Snd it was much quicker going down-hill over a now-familiar path. Both Marcus and his grandfather had much to contemplate. They stopped briefly at the Claron Falls Inn for a late mid-day meal, arriving at the castle just as darkness fell. Marcus had a class to teach the next day, a sixth-day.

CHAPTER

ELEVEN

The trainees seemed happy to see his return. Marcus was relentless, as usual. But his mind was elsewhere. He was actually pleased to receive another note from Katrina as classes concluded for the day. As before, it was a request to meet that night, usual time and place. She was there, waiting, when he arrived.

"How was your camping trip?" she asked.

"You know we went camping? Are there no secrets in this castle?"

"Not from me!" she said, laughing. Then more seriously: "Especially when Kelson tells us where you and the Lord High-mage had gone. So, how was it?"

"Dark. Wet. But at least we ate well. My grandfather was a better cook than I imagined. So what's new here? What's the latest with Sinifir and Prince Stephen?"

Katrina's countenance fell. "Noting good, I can assure you. Sinifir has gone forward with his training. Everyone is now sworn to serve the King, and to keep their association a secret. Your three friends..."

"Ivan, Greta and Thomas?"

"Yes, those three. Are you still sure they can be trusted?"

"Yes, I believe so. Of course, anything could happen. But yes, I believe so. I have a way of contacting them. And now that I'm back, I should. I'll say this, Sinifir is acting swiftly to get them trained."

"Yes to that. And I hope he hasn't planned any 'trial runs' in the next few seven-days. I wonder when he will be making the big moves against my father and your grandfather."

"Remember the envoy to Caldonia? My grandfather and your father think that would provide the ideal opportunity to initiate hostilities. Either kill the envoy, or better, assassinate someone in the royal family. And somehow shift the blame to him."

"Well, that certainly does make sense. Fortunately, Prince Stephen and Sinifir constantly confide in each other. And still consider my brother's quarters the ideal place to do so. Let's hope we get some advanced warning of their plans." She repeated herself: "And as I said, I worry about Sinifir's possible plans for a 'practice exercise' with his assassins before the main event."

"I'm sure he will. We, or I, must be prepared to frustrate it."

Again she stretched up to give Marcus a chaste peck on the cheek. "Later, cousin."

"Second cousin."

"Yes, but cousins still the same." She disappeared into the shrubbery.

The next day was a seventh, and Marcus went to the military training area to look for messages from his three friends. To no surprise, there was a note from Ivan asking for a meeting. They had previously decided to do so on seventh-days, unless an emergency arose. There was a mead house close to the same west gate Marcus had passed through earlier in the seven-day, where they had agreed to meet. Marcus was careful to disguise his departure, wearing the now-worn and hooded seal-skin cape over older clothes. As arranged, he arrived at the mead house at twilight He approached through an indirect path and found the three sitting in a dimly-lit corner, with flagons of mead before them.

"'Bout time yuh got here," said Thomas. "Much later and we might'a been too deep in our drink to recognize yuh." The other two, Ivan and Greta, laughed.

"Don't listen to him," said Greta. "We just barely got here ourselves. I guess you know you're no longer obligated for more training."

"So I heard. It seems Sinifir perceived somehow that I might be a mage. And had doubts about having full control over my actions."

"We figured as much," said Ivan.

'We're down to seven. Want to know who else is in, who's out?"

"I already know. No surprises, except one."

"Who would that be?" asked Greta.

"You" responded Marcus. "I thought you vowed never to take another life."

"I haven't killed anyone yet, Marcus. And I won't. Doesn't mean I can't stick around and see what develops. Besides, these two need me around to protect them."

"That's a guddun" laughed Thomas. Ivan adding their own.

"So, has he sworn you to any kind of loyalty or secrecy yet?"

Greta answered. "Yes, both. Fortunately, he swore us to the King, not to himself. Otherwise we would have walked. We're doing more dagger work, learning quick killing strokes, and how to make people die silently. If there were any question about becoming assassins, there is doubt no longer. It's sad that no one seems to object. Well, except for us, and we're keeping it quiet."

"What a relief! I can give you an alert on what's to come. Jared, the Crown Prince, has sent an envoy to Caldonia with a request to meet here, in Alexa. Presumably to confront and deny rumors of hostility between the two kingdoms. It is expected that Sinifir will seize the opportunity to generate some kind of war, probably assassinate someone royal and push the blame to the envoy."

The three sat quietly, nodding as Marcus spoke.

"That won't be taking place for a many seven-days, at the earliest. What Sinifir is likely to do, though, is to give his assassins some real training. So keep your eyes and ears open. He will likely go after a friend of the royals, but not someone in the royal household itself. One of us will have to intervene. I have no reluctance to do so. And if *I* do it, it would not throw suspicion back on any of you."

With nothing more to discuss, they agreed to disband until the next seventh. Thomas suggested a different inn, to which they all agreed. They left separately and took different routes from the inn in their departures.

The following seven-day was a quiet routine. Training in style and strategy, like the previous defensive training, involved a demonstration by Marcus, followed by slow, careful mimicking by the trainees. Mistakes, however minor, were noted and shown to the class. Once *everyone* had the move down correctly, it was repeated and repeated, at an ever increasing pace. With speed, came errors, so it was back to the beginning again. Marcus drove into the trainees what Kelson had so frequently taught: *practice makes permanent. Only perfect practice produces perfect performance.*

Each night, after the evening meal, Marcus copied more of the Chronicle pages written in *Kult*. It was tedious pen-work, character by character. He had no means of translating words into *Turga*. Nevertheless, he pored over Kentuck's dictionary in an attempt to find the simpler words. In doing so, he discovered the majority of *Kurt* words in the dictionary were those of common conversation, such as those found in stories and ballads.

This made sense, of course. The same literature was available in Turga, so correlating the two was straightforward. Marcus paid special attention to words to which Kentuck had attached commentary. These tended to have special meaning in the context of *gift*. The word for flame, was FO. The word for light was LU. The words for casting them were fo-see-AH and lu-see-AH. He guessed the latter part of the word, the *see-AH* part, had something to do with the command to *cast*. Was it necessary, or could flame and light be cast without the word to do so? He formed an image of flame, mentally placed it in the flame pit, and projected *FO*. Flame appeared in the pit, as it had so many times before.

Having a small amount of *earth-gift*, Saul had known the *Kult* word for exercising his endowment: *tier*. Kentuck had made an extensive commentary on it, making it clear that it was *the* fundamental word associated with the exercise of *earth-gift*. Kentuck had gone on to say that *tier* was closely related to the word for wind, *aer*, and water, *kwer*. Marcus resolved to test his strength in both in the next new-moon cycle.

Another word of power in the dictionary was *pwert*. It had an entire page of commentary, one of the longest Kentuck had written. In simple terms, *pwert* was the power to create a portal between two places. It was its own type of *gift-power*. And those very few who possessed it were highly regarded. However, the power to *pwert* from one place to another expended a considerable amount of *gift-power*. The longer the distance the more consumed. The actual mechanics of porting, the common reference to using *pwert*, could only occur between two places the casting mage had physically visited. Why? Because the mage had to have a clear image, a *very* clear image, in his mind of the porting destination. There were many precautions. Kentuck repeatedly emphasizing that porting was one of the most hazardous endowments of *gift*. Mages were known to port away and never return. It was believed that porting to an ill-defined location led to their disappearance.

Marcus wondered. *How would you know for sure, if they never came back? Puert* would be another word reserved for a new-moon.

"Grandfather?"

"Yes, Marcus."

"What can you tell me about *emergence?*"

"*Gift* emergence? Well, it usually occurs at or soon *after* the transition from childhood, when the body goes through its natural changes. Never earlier. Except in your case, perhaps. But sometimes later. The general thought is that if there has been no emergence by the age of two hands, there is no additional *gift* within the person to emerge. Why do you ask?"

"Do you know Crown Prince Jared's daughter, Katrina?"

"Of course. Sweet girl. Very serious, though. Rarely laughs. She's in your blade-training class, right?"

"Yes, she is. Best trainee I have, in fact.'"

"It was an unusual choice for her Strange for any young girl for that matter. Her father was against it, as you can imagine. But she was determined. I suppose in that regard, she's much like her father: once Jared gets his mind fixed on something, it's just about impossible to get him to change. Do you suspect she's emerging?"

"Emerged, actually. I can sense *gift* in her. Not yet strong, but definitely there."

"Well, there should be no surprise. Her great grandfather's brother, my wife's uncle, was remarkably strong in *gift*. As was your grandmother, Susanna. Just looks like it skipped a generation or two, or three. Not that unusual, I suppose. Do you want me to mention it to her father? Or at least, have her tested?"

"I think not. I'm not sure making it known to Sinifir and her brother, Prince Stephen, would be a good idea at this time. I believe it would make her a bigger target than she already is."

"Yes, I suppose you are right about that. Keep me advised, though, on how she develops."

Marcus searched out Kelson before classes were to begin. The trainees were taking the customary morning laps around the training compound following their *tai kai* exercises.

"Lord Kelson, do you have a moment, sir?"

"Of course, Marcus. What can I do for you? Your class is going acceptably?"

"Yes sir. I'm very pleased with their progress. They did well the time they were with you. But I have a request."

"What would that be?"

"I would like to introduce a little variety into their training. Would you allow me to begin their training on casting?"

"Blade casting?"

"Yes sir. I know it is a bit early, while they are still working with long-blades. But casting was always something I looked forward to and enjoyed. I think they would respond well to the variety and challenge."

Kelson thought for a moment. "I can see no reason against it. I'll drop down to the armory and tell them you will be picking up casting blades. When do you plan on starting? And where would you like to do it?"

"I was thinking today. I would take them over to the casting gallery after the mid-day meal. Of course, their main focus will continue to be on long-blades. So casting would be, say, three half-days each seven? Does that sound acceptable?"

"Sounds good to me. I don't know of anyone using the casting alleys these days. If you want, I'll pick up the blades and have them ready after mid-day. Do you want me to address the students?"

"Certainly, if you wish. You are always welcome in my class. As you well know. But if you don't have time, I'm happy to get them started."

Marcus didn't tell the trainees any particulars, except that there would be a change in their training schedule after mid-day meal. They followed him over to the casting gallery, where numerous wooden and straw targets were set. There were eight narrow hand casting "alleys" separated from each other by sturdy wooden panels a hand of hands high. Any ricochets would not imperil other trainees.

As expected, Kelson was there waiting, a pile of casting blades on the table before him. "Welcome trainees!" he said in a happy voice. "Your instructor, Marcus, thought you would enjoy a bit of variety. So he has suggested you might like trying your hand at blade casting."

A murmur of excitement passed through the trainees.

"Marcus, perhaps you might want to demonstrate a few times for the class?" He turned to the trainees. "I've seen how well he does it. I have no doubt you have a capable teacher. Marcus, if you please?"

Marcus picked up a blade and led the class to the closest alley. He stood about three paces from the target, a wooded shield painted with concentric circles. There was a heart at its center. He slipped the blade from his left hand to his right. With a sudden motion, he cast and buried it in target's heart. He gave the throw a little boost and nudge with *gift*, wanting to make sure his first impression would be a lasting one. The students let out a collective gasp. It had happened so quickly, and apparently with so little effort, that it caught them by total surprise.

"Well done, Marcus. Well done." Turning to the class, Kelson continued. "I'm sure, soon enough, you will all be equally adept." He departed with a little laugh and a flick of his hand in farewell.

"Attention, class. Gather around. Blade-casting takes a great deal of practice. The key is to throw the blade without spin. Yes, there are some blade-casters who learn how to throw with one-half spin, or a full spin, or a spin and half. But that is *not* how we will learn to cast. Throwing without spin will allow you to have the same casting motion for any distance. Let me show you what I mean." Marcus was now farther from the target than before, nearly six paces. Again he threw, with the same result as before. Another murmur of amazement arose from the trainees. "What I just did takes much practice. Like blade work, it might be many turnings, even turns, before you become so adept. All that starts here, today. So we will begin with the proper way to hold a casting-blade."

The trainees arranged themselves in a tight arc two paces before him. "Heretofore we've only used wooden training blades. This is your first work with actual weapons. The blades we will be using are the exact blades used in combat. Please, each of you carefully select a blade from the table." The students were quick to do so and to return to their positions. "Casting blades is different from how other blades are used. You obviously see they are sharply pointed. They have no handles, save the flat portion of the blade itself. And no sharpened edge. They are designed to penetrate, not cut, and appear very simply made. But I assure you they are carefully balanced and made of hardened steel. The secret to throwing without spin is in *how* you hold the blade, and the *method* you use in casting it. We will begin with the grip."

Once the trainees had been shown the correct way to hold the blade, the blade held firmly against the middle finger, he demonstrated the correct throw. It was more of a horizontal casting motion, similar to the way a spear would be thrown. When they could copy his moves, he had them each retrieve three additional blades and pair up, two-by-two, in consecutive casting alleys.

"Now, I want you all to take a position two paces from the target. Watch each other carefully. The first to throw will take blade in hand and prepare to cast. The other will observe and critique form. The idea is that you learn to recognize the correct method in someone other than yourself, learning how to do it better in the process. I will be watching and correcting as well. Do not be surprised if your attempts fail. Actually," he said with a chuckle, "be surprised if your attempts do *not* fail."

Casting began in all eight stalls. It was obvious the trainees were enjoying themselves. There was mixed success, from very poor to poor, with one exception. After a few bad results, Katrina seemed to get the grip and motion down and began embedding her blades cleanly into the target. Marcus had maneuvered the class into short-blade casting for this specific purpose. He had watched her rapid development with long-blades. If his suspicions were correct, Katrina's endowment was as a battle-mage. After some practice, his suspicions were confirmed. Marcus moved her training partner into a threesome and asked her to help him with the others.

When classes concluded, he whispered to her as they passed. "Tonight?" She gave a subtle nod.

They entered the palm garden simultaneously, but from different directions. Katrina was the first to speak. "That was fun. We do it again, right?"

"Yes. First-, third- and fifth-days. After the mid-day meal."

"I'm looking forward to it!" she exclaimed, silently clapping her hands.

"There's something you need to know. Something I've suspected for a while, something you confirmed for me today."

She gave him a puzzled look.

"Your *gift* has emerged. I believe you are, or eventually will become, a battle-mage."

She looked at him speechless. Finally she regained her voice. "And you say this because?"

"Katrina, you know I'm strong in *gift*. Probably an equal to Sinifir. But please, let's keep that between us. He and I can sense *gift* in others. It's why he dropped me from his list of potential assassins. You heard him say as much. There are, or were, several reasons to think you would become a battle-mage. First, I've sensed the emergence of your *gift*. Second, our particular endowment is established long before we emerge. It moves us in the direction our *gift* will eventually take. You have always held a fascination for combat. And persuaded your father, Crown Prince Jared, to let you train as a blades-man. Your skill with the long-blade has progressed remarkably, especially in the last turning. It only remained for you to be tested."

"And that is what this blade-casting is all about? A ruse just to test me?"

"Yes. But for what it's worth, it's valuable training for everyone. And it appears they are enjoying it immensely."

"So. If you are right, and I have emerged as a *what-ever*, let's say *battle-mage*, where does that take me, take us?"

"Mixed situation. If Sinifir senses your *gift*, he will make you an even earlier target. Dark mages fear but few things: a stronger mage, or a weaker mage with a threatening *gift*. A battle-mage would certainly be a matter of concern. Fortunately, as your *gift*-power strengthens, you will be in a better position to defend yourself, both mentally and physically. I'm going to teach you how to protect yourself from his mind-touch. And physically, I've brought you these."

Marcus handed her the small bundle he had been carrying. She unwrapped it to find his two black daggers, those given to him during his assassin training. "I know Captain Morris wanted these back. But I was out with my grandfather when he came around to collect them. He hasn't said anything since, so I assume it's slipped his mind. I want you to have them and practice blade casting. They are a lot harder to control than the throwing blades you used today. But I am sure you will soon be the master of them."

"Thank you, Marcus. You have given me much to think about."

"You are welcome. Before you go, we need to talk about mind-touch. Sinifir is constantly touching and probing the minds of others. He looks for any opportunity to influence. And he looks for threats. He cannot do this from a distance. So when you are near him, and feel any kind of compulsion or persuasion, you must focus your mind on something specific. Close your mind to anything else. I suggested that my three friends think of a brick wall. I t seemed to work for them. And again, stay as far from Sinifir as you can."

"Like I said, you've given me much to think about." She gave him her usual peck on the cheek, turned, and was gone.

CHAPTER

TWELVE

By day, Marcus taught. Later, he spent long evenings copying the chronicles written in *Kurt*, still studying Kentuck's dictionary. Working through the entries in the dictionary tended to raise as many questions as it answered. Marcus kept returning to the three words that intrigued him the most: *tier* (earth), *puert* (port), and *tiemp* (time). His grandfather only had experience with *tier* and its related words *aer* (air) and *kwer* (water).

"Water and air are difficult to control, Marcus, because they have no particular form. So earth-mages that have the *gift* to manipulate them, really can't do much more than steer the flow that already exists. They are called wind-mages and water-mages. Except wind-mages are nearly always women. No, I don't know why. So sailors refer to them as *wind-witches*. Men are called *wind-wizards*. Like all strong mages, wind-mages are rare. You hear stories about them from sailors, wind-witches who would stand at the bow of a ship and re-direct the wind to the benefit of the sails. In a heavy gale, sailors were known to lash a wind-witch to the ship's mast to keep her from blowing overboard. While she did her best to keep the ship afloat. Naturally, any wind-mage who could make ships go faster and safer during heavy weather would be greatly sought after and highly esteemed."

"And water mages?" asked Marcus.

"Yes, they are like wind-witches in a way. But water, being much heavier, is harder to manipulate. For the most part, all that a water mage can do is influence how the water flows, one way or the other. Currents in the sea are much larger than river currents. So a water-mage is quite useless for sailors on, say, the Betting Sea. But for river craft, water-mages can be quite useful, especially in moving smaller boats and river craft around dock yards and piers."

"Can water and air be pulled or pushed with *gift*, beyond the ability to just move its direction? I mean, can *gift* actually *create* movement, rather than simply steering a flow that already exists?"

"I assume you mean, for example, create a wind that otherwise wasn't there. Or cause still water to flow? Well, Marcus, those are interesting questions indeed. The answers to which, unfortunately, is 'I haven't a clue'."

"What about just reaching for water and pulling it out of the ground? Wouldn't that be the same thing as causing still water to flow?"

"That would be a great ability, Marcus. Especially if you were traveling and there were no rivers or streams near by. I would think, though, if it *were* possible, it would take a great deal of *gift-power* to move water through solid ground."

"Then how about this. If an earth-mage, or say, a water-mage, *could* make water come out of the ground, is there any reason he or she couldn't move other things to the surface, like silver or gold? You know, just summon them forth from the ground? You said the ancients did that with the great foundation stones that underlie the capitol cities."

Saul let out a sigh. "Marcus, I have no idea what a truly powerful earth-mage could or could not do. I suppose if the mage could imagine it, with enough *gift-power* he or she could make it happen. Subject to the laws of *gift* and nature itself, of course. A mage limited only by his or her imagination. Now *that's* a frightening thought indeed, is it not?"

Marcus nodded. "I think it's time to go to bed."

"I agree. Sometimes you make my mind spin with all your questions."

Marcus retired to his bedroom and to his bed. *Just some more things to try on the next full-moon.*

Marcus had kept careful track of the days that passed. On seventh-days he had continued to meet with Ivan, Greta and Thomas. They had little to report, beyond their continued training. As predicted, they were learning about killing blows, potions and poisons. They were having second thoughts about even continuing, finding nothing in their studies that gave them pleasure or joy. But, by consensus, they agreed to continue simply for its intelligence benefit. No 'assignments' as such had been issued.

Likewise, daily training with his hand and six trainees had fallen into a routine of long-blades, six days each seven, and short blades three half-days after mid-day meal. Progress with the young students was constant. Katrina continued to excel in both.

The new moon approached, its peak falling on a second-day soon after the mid-day meal. Marcus became more and more anxious to test his theory, that it simply took more *gift power* to unlock the abilities of which he had read. There was one complication in his plan to return to the Claron wilderness. His grandfather would be unable to go with him. In a way, Marcus was relieved that he would be going alone. Some of the things he wanted to attempt might not meet with grandfather's approval. And if he were successful, he may want to keep it to himself.

He asked Kelson for an additional four days off 'for personal reasons'. Kelson was reluctant, but relented. Unlike other instructors, Marcus had made few demand. And by all accounts, was one of the better teachers, certainly among the most popular.

It was the seventh day before the next new moon. "So you are going in the morning? Do you feel safe in doing so by yourself?" asked Saul.

"Yes. I'm not concerned with the trip itself, just what might happen during the *gift* flow. But I'm taking precautions with that. I'm pretty sure I will be fine."

"What precautions?" asked Saul.

"Well, we learned that if I'm not actually in contact with the earth, the flow stops. So I am going to arrange my pack in such a way that if I'm beginning to feel overwhelmed, I'll just roll on to it and break the connection. I'll have to be careful, though."

"Sounds like that should work. You're going to be all right with food and cooking?"

"Yes, I remember what you showed me." *Not to mention everything I learned in siege training.* "I'll be looking for smaller game, though, since I'll only be cooking for myself."

Marcus had prepared a written list of the things he wanted to try, both before and after the new-moon event. He left early on first-day, the pack heavier than before since he had to bear the entirety of the camping gear, plus food and cooking utensils. If he stayed the full four days, it would be a day longer than they had stayed before. He thought of finding a different place, perhaps closer to the city. But discretion prevailed. And if there were problems, his grandfather would know where to find him. The way was familiar and by mid-day Marcus had passed beyond Claron Falls. He only paused for a brief lunch and a refill of his water flagon.

Less than a league beyond the Falls, in a rather dense patch of forest, Marcus encountered a group of four frightened hunters. They were scrambling their way back toward the village.

"Be really careful, young man. We were hunting mountain bear. And unfortunately, we found a big one. We only wounded him, and now we are fleeing from his wrath. We've been hearing him thrashing around behind us in pursuit. You'd best be coming back with us."

Marcus gave it some thought. He was well armed with a cross-bow, a long-blade, and the two short-blades Kelson had given him. And with his *gift-power,* should be safe. "Thank you for the warning. But there's a place I have to be. So I guess I will be on my way."

The hunters tried again to persuade Marcus to return with them, to no avail. Finally, with a collective shrug, they broke off their pleadings and continued on in the direction of Claron Falls.

Marcus knew that a wounded animal was always more dangerous. A wounded forest bear, of large size no less, had to be taken seriously. He loosened the long-blade in its scabbard. But with a heavy pack on his shoulders, it was not a weapon he could quickly draw. He moved forward with caution, making as little sound as possible. After some time, Marcus sensed a change in the forest. It had grown silent. Gone were the twitter of birds and the chirps and whistles of squirrels. Even insect noises had seemed to disappear. He could feel the hackles of hair on his neck rise. Without warning, six paces in front of him, a huge, hairy animal burst from the undergrowth and bounded straight for him. Without any time to draw a weapon, Marcus instinctively raised his hands and drew the bear's life force to himself. The bear collapsed forward, and tumbled to an unmoving mass of flesh and fur a scant pace before him. A combination of shock and the influx of the bear's life-force dropped Marcus to his knees.. "By the *fata,* what have I just done?"

He had killed. For the first time, Marcus knew he had used his *gift*-power to take a creature's life. He looked forlornly at the beast at his feet, feeling both relief and sorrow. The beast had two arrows protruding from its back. And a broken shaft was hanging from its shoulder. It had been wounded and was angry and in pain. And now it was dead. Virtue number three.

Marcus placed his pack on the ground and sat upon it. Bear meat was tough and unpleasant. The hunters had pursued it for the sole purpose of adventure. The excitement of a hunt. The taking of a trophy hide. Was he of the same disposition? If so, would he use his *gift* again in such a blood-lust? The third virtue of the *fata* came suddenly to his mind. *Do not wantonly take the life of man or beast.* With a relief, he looked inside himself and found only sorrow. For now, he was not inclined to the dark side of *gift*.

The magnificent beast deserved better than to be eaten by carrion. Marcus imagined a deep pit next to the bear, invoked *tier*, and cast power. A large hole opened, into which he rolled the carcass. He then imagined earth returning to cover the bear, cast *tier* once again, and proceeded to pull leaves and twigs over the grave. "I return you to the earth, from whence cometh all life." Marcus shouldered his pack and resumed his journey. After a short while, the sounds of the forest returned.

Marcus had come across a bevy of quail during the post midday trek. He had quietly slipped off his pack, withdrawn his crossbow, and killed a pair. He had then plucked and field dressed them, wrapping them in leaves as his grandfather had shown. He arrived at the campsite just as the sun slipped below the trees. The glade was unchanged. The burn-pit he had built the cycle before was as it had been left. The "grave" depression he had created was intact, though the edges had begun to erode. He unpacked the tent and ground cloth and prepared them for the night. A short time later the quail were roasting over hot coals. And the same tasty bulbs he and his grandfather had eaten before were boiling in the pot. As he ate, Marcus thought through the activities he had planned for the morrow. He retired to his bedroll and slept surprisingly well.

Being encamped on the west side of the glade, the sun rose early above the tree-line to the east. Marcus made his way to the small stream below the campsite, bathed himself, and drank deeply of the clear, cold water. A breakfast of roasted quail and re-warmed vegetables was brief, but filling. He examined his list of 'experiments'. How else to describe them? He selected *kwer*, the *gift* endowment to influence water. He returned to the stream and imagined the water flowing more swiftly on one side of the stream than the other. Once it was clearly in his mind, he mentally bespoke *kwer* and cast power. To his surprise, the stream did change, moving just as he had imagined. The unequal flow created curious patterns in the middle of the stream. He again invoked *kwer*, imagining it returning to its original flow. He now turned his attention to the more difficult task, not just of changing the existing flow of water, but the creation of new flow. Using *tier* he created a small depression in the ground two paces from the stream. Kneeling by the shallow hole, he placed his hands on its bottom and imagined it filling with water. When he had the vision of it firmly in mind, he cast *kwer* into the ground. He waited. Nothing seemed to be happening, though he thought he had felt a flow of power. He was about to give up, when he felt his finger grow moist. Slowly at first, then faster and faster, the depression began to fill. When full, Marcus lifted his hands and the flow of water ceased. And it had taken a surprisingly small amount of *gift*.

Both amazed and satisfied, Marcus decided to try *aer*. He returned to his camp and sat on a stone he had retrieved the previous cycle. It was near the burn-pit, which still contained smoldering coals. He rekindled the flame with a few small, dry sticks then placed several green, leafy branches on top. Almost immediately they began to heat, then burn. In the calm of morning, a pillar of steam-gray smoke rose straight into the sky above. Marcus took several paces back, imagined the smoke moving in his direction, and invoked *aer*. Abruptly, the rising smoke shifted to him, encompassing him in an acrid embrace. Coughing, he returned the smoke to its prior flow.

Marcus turned to the more difficult task. He imagined in his mind a wind-twist, such as he had seen on dry, hot third-turning days. He had been fascinated by the way they could sweep up grass and leaves, even small sticks, and lift them high into the air, to disappear over the castle walls. He fixed this image firmly in his mind, trying to recall all of the details he had observed. When he was satisfied, he closed his eyes, spoke the word *aer*, and simultaneously cast *gift*. Unlike the experiment with water, the effect on air was immediate, and much stronger than expected. The wind-twist whipped at his clothing and snatched the tent and ground cloth from their pegs. Marcus quickly released the wind-twist and went in pursuit of tent and ground cloth, which had been raised some distance from the ground and carried nearly three-hand paces to the east. And fortunately, they went east, or Marcus would have been climbing trees to retrieve them.

It was late morning, the time approaching for the new-moon flux of *gift*. Marcus sat and waited. Eventually, after mid-day came and went, he felt the surge of *gift* begin. He got up and placed his pack at his side, ready for an immediate escape if needed. The surge continued to grow, and at last the gorge came. Marcus stretched forth his arms and pulled *gift* to himself. The response was immediate and profound. When he was about to be overwhelmed, Marcus rolled over to sit on his pack. But to no avail! *Gift-power* continued to flow. Marcus was terrified. His skin began to itch and burn, his vision blurred. He tried to cast the overwhelming surge of *gift* back into the earth. But it seemed merely to rebound back to him.

At the moment of total despair, as Marcus was slipping into unconsciousness, the surge began to subside. Then stopped completely. He lay gasping, hurting everywhere. His stomach voided. Dazed, he gave thought to what had occurred. First, moving to the pack had not worked. Two, he had survived the full brunt of a new-moon surge. Three, he had never sensed as full of *gift* as he now felt. He took a series of deep breaths, doing his best to stand. Eventually he succeeded, and made his way to the tent where the flagon of water had been placed. He felt better after a deep drink. But remained weakened by the trauma of *gift-sickness*. Sleep. He needed sleep. He sank down to the ground cloth and slept.

When Marcus woke, it was morning. Again. Had he been out for one night, or two? He had no way of knowing. He desperately needed to void, and was ravenously hungry. He took care of the first, and began searching for something edible to satisfy the second. He would have to hunt. But for now, bulbs would suffice. Fortunately, they were plentiful and near at hand. He ate several raw while others simmered in the cooking pot. His skin was again reddened and had begun to itch and peal. But otherwise, he felt fine. Perhaps even better than fine.

The meal finished, Marcus went in pursuit of game. He stretched out his mind-touch and detected life at the far end of the glade. Cross-bow in hand, he headed in that direction, finding a small colony of rabbits browsing in the tall grasses. He cast a bolt at a particularly large buck, using *gift* to direct it to its target. Marcus was clearly stronger in *gift*. The bolt did not waver in the least and sped with such velocity that it went completely through the animal and buried itself deeply in the ground beyond. Marcus retrieved the bolt, finding its shaft splintered. He field dressed and skinned the rabbit and returned to the campsite. He piled sticks on the cold ashes (how long had he slept, he wondered), carefully cast flame, and soon had the rabbit roasting over hot coals. Without ceremony, he plucked pieces of simmering meat from the spit and ate his fill.

There were two tests remaining: *puert* and *tiemp*, porting and the manipulation of time. He chose to work on *puert* first. His understanding of porting was that a destination had to be *clearly* imagined in his mind, a place he had personally visited and of which he had a clear recollection. Marcus had already given this much thought. He chose a destination close at hand, the place on the stream where he had frequently gone for water. He had taken careful note of the place, the bank, the depth of water, and the stones over which the water flowed. With that image clearly in his mind, and concentrating to his fullest, Marcus invoked the word *puert* and cast *gift*.

Marcus did not know what to expect, so when a doorway – of sorts – opened before him, with a clear image beyond of the flowing stream, he was at a loss of what to do. Losing concentration, the doorway faded away. He tried again, forming the same image in his mind and casting while invoking *pert*. This time, after the doorway appeared, he walked through, finding himself standing by the stream about three-hand paces from where he stood a few moments before. *Gif* had been used, but very little. Marcus had read, though, that the amount of *gift* required for porting depended strongly on the distances involved. But however short the distance, Marcus had successfully ported. The test was complete.

The final test was one of manipulating time. Try as he would, using every way he could imagine it escaped him. After an exhausting time of trying, he gave up the attempt.

It was growing late in the day. Marcus slew another rabbit and pulled more bulbs. He ate and went to bed. He was tired. He slept well.

A heavy storm swept in during the night. Marcus awoke early, rolled up the tent and ground cloth and made ready his trek back to the castle. On a whim, he conjured up a clear image of his room, a room he knew so very well. He cast *gift* and the door appeared. He felt a drain of *gift* as he walked through, slightly more than the first time he had ported. But it was worth it. He was home. He removed his wet clothing and left his room. His grandfather was sitting at the table having breakfast. "Well! When did you get back? It must have been late, I didn't hear you come in."

Marcus started to say something about porting, but hesitated. Perhaps his ability to port was something he wasn't quite ready to share? "I have kind of lost track of days, grandfather. It is fourth-day, right?"

"Fourth-day? No, it's fifth day. You have classes today, right?"

So I slept a full day with my gift-sickness. *A night, a day, and a night. It's a good thing I ported home.* "Yes, and it looks like I've overslept. I have to hurry, or I'm going to be late."

"Before you go, you look a little... sunburned?"

"Yes, I spent too much time in that open glade of ours. I should have covered myself up a bit better." He was sure his grandfather saw through his excuse. But nothing more was said. Marcus hurried through a small-bath, dressed, and went off to the training fields.

CHAPTER

THIRTEEN

Being a fifth-day, the post mid-day class involved the casting of short-blades. During his absence, Kelson had not followed Marcus' schedule, but chose instead to have the class work exclusively on long-blades. Marcus knew why, but did not disclose the reason to the class. Kelson was not skilled at casting. The students enthusiastically assembled in the casting gallery when the mid-day meal was behind them. Marcus had invited them to also practice in the evening after classes, if they were so inclined. The arms-master had been advised. He had no objection to dispensing blades, provided they were all returned as they left for the night. He had quarters within the armory, so after-meal requests were no burden. Provided the requests were indeed *after* his last-meal.

To Marcus' trained eye, it was clear who had been practicing and who had not. The ones who had spent evenings with casting blades were the worst in the class or the best; the former in hopes of catching up with the others, the latter because they enjoyed the challenge. Katrina was in the second, and her skill was nothing short of remarkable. He caught her attention and she sidled up to him. "You are doing really well. How are things going, you know, in general?"

"There are important things to talk about. Tonight, as usual." It was more a statement than question.

"I'll be there. How are you doing with ... the other blades?"

"That's one of the things we need to talk about."

They separated. Marcus continued with teaching, Katrina with practice, and helping other trainees from time to time.

Marcus debated bringing Katrina into his confidence. In the end, he realized she was the only absolutely sure ally he had, except for his grandfather of course/ And possibly Crown Prince Jared. But he didn't know the Crown Prince, except for the few times they had met. Besides, she was a cousin, and what greater loyalty could there be, besides family? Well, Prince Stephen excepted. There were also the three friends, Ivan, Greta and Thomas. But they would neither understand nor appreciate the nuances of *gift*. Decision made, he waited until it grew dark, then ported from his room to the palm garden. Katrina was there waiting, perched on a stone bench. When he suddenly appeared through the portal, she was barely able to suppress a scream of alarm and fright. Marcus stepped up, placed a first-finger over her lips, and gave her a *shushing* sound. In a low voice. "It's something new I've learned to do with *gift*, Keep it between us." Katrina nodded in reply, surprise still evident in her eyes. "So tell me, Katrina, what has been happening during my absence?"

The question seemed to bring Katrina out of shock and back into focus. "Not good. As you suspected, Sinifir has decided to try out the skills, and dare I say, commitment, of his new assassins. Well, the most promising of the lot."

"Let me guess. Louton or Camden?"

"Louton is still too rough, needs more... refinement. Yes, Camden. Sinifir has him 'on a leash like a dog'. He makes light of it, privately, when he is with Stephen."

"Do you know who the victim is going to be, and when?"

"Not someone I know. It's a merchant, by the name of Abbott. Do you know him?"

"No, well, yes, I know *of* him. He's one of the richer tradesmen here in Alexa. He and my grandfather have been friends for many turns. He's always been a very loyal kings-man. I wonder why Sinifir would target him."

"There seems to have been some falling out between them/ Something about an exchange of goods. At first, Abbott agreed to take everything on consignment and resell it. But then Abbott backed out after suspecting it to be stolen. And he wasn't quiet about his suspicions. Sinifir denied it, of course, but felt his reputation had been tarnished."

"Was there anything to Abbott's suspicions?"

"I don't know for sure. Knowing Sinifir? Probably. In any case, Camden was instructed to 'put him down' on this seventh-day evening. Apparently, Abbott is a bit of a religious sort. Or more likely, a good friend to the monks. He faithfully goes to the *fata* chapel of an early post mid-day. And after considerable time of camaraderie and a 'wee bit of drink' he returns, usually quite late. You know where the chapel is, right? Lots of dark alleys along that way back to his home."

"Yes, I know the way." He thought of Kentuck the Crazy. "I had a friend that lived just beyond. And you are right, not the best of neighborhoods."

"So what are we going to do?"

"We? You've done your part. Now it's time for me to do mine."

"But..."

"No *buts*, Katrina. This will be between us *assassins*."

She thought for a moment and nodded. "You're right, Marcus. It's out of my expertise. I know, no *buts*, but please be careful." With that she gave him the usual peck on the check. "Umm, may I see you port away?"

Marcus chuckled quietly. He opened a portal back to his bedroom and stepped through.

Today was a sixth and Marcus was glad to see the seven-day draw to a close. There was a note from the three, asking for a meeting on *sixth*-night, that very night. He memorized the location, tore the note in small pieces, and scattered them along the way home. He would be out late tonight, and surely the night to follow. It had already been a difficult seven-day. He had looked forward to his first good night's sleep in nearly a full seven-day. But it wouldn't be until the next first-day, at the earliest. He might be able to take a nap, before he met the three? Unfortunately, his grandfather was waiting his return.

"Marcus, you haven't told me anything about your little trip this seven-day. And I can tell the difference between sunburn and *gift* sickness. So, what happened? Did you experience the new-moon flow?"

"Yes, and when the surge came, and I thought I had had enough, I rolled over to my pack. But it didn't stop anything! I survived the full flow. And I was so overwhelmed that I slept the rest of the day and the next as well."

"And that's why you asked me what day it was?"

"Yes. I didn't know how long I had slept. So I just left, and came home. Got here late, then overslept."

"I saw the wet clothes you left by the flame to dry."

"Yes, it rained. The trip back was, well, different."

"Yes, I suppose it would be. We had a hard rainfall here as well. Did you eat acceptably well?"

"Quail the first day, then rabbit. Both were quite tasty, if I say so myself."

"What about, what about the things you wanted to try? With *gift*."

"Not what I expected. A few little things. Couldn't do anything with *tiemp*." He sighed. 'And that was what I was most curious about. Actually, grandfather, after the *gift* sickness, I backed off a bit. Maybe next cycle I'll make another effort. So, I guess that's all I have for you." *Not all I have, just all I have for you.*

"Well, glad to have you home and safe. But I don't know about you going off alone again."

"I do have a question, though. It's about the new-moon flux of *gift*. The first time my *gift* sickness was so severe I almost died. This time, I went through the whole event. Yes, I got *gift* sickness again. But I survived it much better. Why is that?"

"I think I answered that question some time ago. Let me explain it again, at least, what I believe happened. A mage's capacity to possess and hold *gift* expands through his or her use of *gift*. I suppose your previous experience with a new-moon flow increased your capacity to *almost* absorb a full flow. Well, that, and some new-moon flows are lighter than others, I don't know why. In any case, you survived. Barely. I'm not sure you should try doing it again without me there to observe. It obviously takes more than sitting on your pack to create an interruption."

"Thank you. That helps. By the way, I'm going out for a walk tomorrow. I thought I would go over to the *fata* chapel and say hello to some of Kentuck's friends. I promised to stop back for a visit/ And that was many seven-days ago. Would that be all right?"

"Of course. It isn't the best of neighborhoods, so be careful." He paused. "Forgive me Marcus. I don't know why I'm telling you that. You are more than capable of defending yourself. Take a cross-bow, anyway. Please."

"Thank you. I shall."

Once his grandfather had retired for the night, Marcus slipped away to join his friends. It was a bit later than usual. His friends had been waiting for some time and made their bother obvious,. They were still in good humor, however. Marcus was not much of a drinker, but he did not refuse the flagon of weak-mead waiting for him.

"Much to tell, Marcus," began Greta, who had evolved into the group's spokesperson. "It is finally going to happen, we believe."

"Camden."

The three looked at each other, their surprise obvious.

"But why would Sinifir make his plans public to the rest of you? It seems against the secret nature of individual assignments."

"You are right, of course. Sinifir only *suggested* there would be individual testing, beginning this seventh-day. But Camden couldn't keep it quiet. We don't know the particulars, but he was boasting about being the *first* to be so tested."

"He didn't say anything about the intended victim?"

The three looked at each other and shook their heads. "No, except that it was someone 'the king' needed to have eliminated. It's 'for the good of the kingdom', of course."

"Well," said Marcus. "Let me remove all doubt about Sinifir's character. I tell you with absolute authority. The intended victim has no issues with the King, nor the King with him. This is a personal issue between Sinifir and the intended target."

Ivan: "And you know this, how?"

Thomas: "Yah. How'sit you know more than we do?"

"I can't tell you that without risking my source. And you can't let Sinifir know we know, without risking all our lives, as well."

Greta: "Don't worry about that, Marcus. We're still tight and firmly against Sinifir. For how much longer? That is anyone's guess. First assignment 'test' and I'm out of the program."

The other two, Ivan and Thomas, echoed her sentiments.

Greta spoke again. "So, what should we do about Camden? We can't let him go through with this assassination, can we?"

"I think I have that in hand. I don't want you involved, though. If things don't go as planned, there's no reason to have your lives shortened. With luck, there will be one fewer member of your merry band of assassins, come first-day morning."

Ivan: "We wish you success. Couldn't happen to a more deserving piece of ... well, you know what I mean."

"Dross. A piece of dross!" said Thomas, with conviction.

With that, they scooted their chairs away from the dark, corner table and took their leave. Marcus made his way quietly, stealthily, back to the castle. His grandfather was sleeping soundly and apparently had not noticed his absence. He undressed and climbed into bed. Notwithstanding the tensions and anxieties of the day, he was soon fast asleep.

Abbott, Marcus knew from prior conversations he had overheard, lived to the east of the castle, in an affluent, well lit, and heavily traveled area of Alexa. The chapel was to the west. Marcus left after his morning meal, taking the same path he had used when searching for Kentuck. This time, he took careful note of the alleys and stretches of empty buildings. Intercepting Camden would be no easy task in the evening, given the many ambush opportunities along the way. Two strategies presented themselves to his mind. Should he intercept Camden before his planned attack? Or follow Abbott closely and intervene before or during the attack itself? With a little thought, Marcus settled on the first. With luck, Abbott would complete his visit to the chapel and return home, none the wiser. Marcus was quite sure he could make the vile Camden disappear without a trace. Let it remain a mystery for Sinifir and Stephen to ponder? They would certainly not make a public issue of his disappearance, either with the Guard or the other trainees. He returned back to the castle.

Marcus did not want to be seen traveling to or from the chapel that evening. So during his morning surveillance he selected and 'memorized' a particularly dark alley within two-hand paces of the chapel itself. Camden would not perform his deadly deed so close to the chapel that a cry might be heard and investigated.

As evening fell, Marcus told his grandfather that he was very, very tired, no lie there, and wanted to retire early. And *please, do not disturb me till morning.* His grandfather acknowledged his request, and promised to be quiet. Marcus closed his bedroom door, securing it from the inside. He then arranged pillows on his cot, making it appear that he was under the coverlets. He donned the darkest clothing he had. He then covered them with his dull-colored hooded cape and ported to his planned hideout.

His chosen location afforded a good view of the street leading to the chapel. Marcus had left early enough to, hopefully, see Abbott's arrival to the chapel. But apparently not. The evening passed into darkness with little foot traffic, none of which stopped at the chapel. Clearly, there were people inside. From his vantage point he could hear occasional voices rise in some form of celebration. Abbott and the monks were apparently enjoying their 'wee bit of drink'.

When it finally grew fully dark, Marcus felt confident Camden had slipped into position. He quietly left his hiding place and began retracing Abbott's path back to the east. Sticking to the shadows, Marcus used mind-touch to search each possible point of ambush. To a casual observer, Marcus was but another traveler passing slowly on his way. Fortunately, after so many seven-days of combat, he knew Camden well, and was able to search for his particular patterns of thought. He was finally successful some six-hand paces from the chapel, in a particularly dark stretch of the lane. Camden had chosen well. Marcus strode past the alley as casually as possible. When out of Camden's sight, he quietly entered the following alley. The alleys were open-ended at this stretch of the road. He was able to turn back and enter the rear of the alley, finding Camden crouched near the entrance, intently focused in the direction of the chapel. Marcus slipped quietly up to him and soundlessly drew one of his short blades. The old-steel passed effortless through Camden's throat. He fell in his death without a sound. Marcus dragged the lifeless body back into the shadows to the rear of the alley. He removed the two daggers Camden carried on his belt, and his meager coin purse as well. As an afterthought, he also removed the boots. They had value to a thief. *No use wasting these. He certainly has no more use for them.* With a nudge of earth-power, Marcus cast a shallow pit for the boots. And with that, he ported back to his bedroom. He stowed the daggers at the bottom-most recesses of his chest and pocketed the coin, a silver and seven coppers. Strangely, he felt no remorse for Camden's death. No remorse at all.

The next two days passed without incident. Marcus was finally able to catch up on the sleep he had lost the previous seven-day. Third-day, after the mid-day meal, was devoted to practice in blade casting. As they were assembling, Katrina slipped up to him. In a small, frightened voice, she whispered. "We need to talk. Stephen searched my room and found your daggers. He was furious. He has made all kinds of outlandish accusations."

Marcus spoke from the corner of his mouth. "What did you tell him?" He took her hand and put a casting-blade into her palm, and demonstrated an under-hand throw. In a voice those nearby could clearly hear, he said "keep trying until you get this down."

Katrina continued in the same small voice. "That you had given them to me for practice. Practice with a different kind of short-blade."

Marcus kept his voice low as well. "Perfect. And that's exactly what I did. If they ask, I'll tell them the same."

"Sinifir is in a rage about Camden. He's been found, murdered and robbed. I've got to go. People are noticing."

Marcus continued the deception. "Now, show me again how to cast under-hand." She did, several times, then returned to a casting alley where she began repeating that same under-hand throw.

Marcus looked up as a man approached. It was Captain Morris. "Captain, what can I do for you today?"

"Where are my daggers? You didn't return them."

"No, but then you never said you wanted them back. I intended to return them to the armory."

"But you didn't."

"No, I brought them with me here. But instead of turning them in, I loaned them to one of the students who asked about casting a more difficult kind of short-blade. I told her to practice with them. And if she *could* find success, she was a better blade-caster than I. She was to turn them into the arms-master when she finished her practices."

"And who was the student?"

"I said 'she' did I not? It was Katrina, the only woman in my class. The one I was just instructing in under-hand throws. We can ask her about them, if you wish."

"No need to disturb her practice now. But you get them back and give them to *me*, not the arms-master."

"I'll do my best. I'll take care of it today."

Captain Morris spun on his heel and left, obviously distressed.

----- OOO -----

After class, Marcus grabbed Katrina's arm as she passed. He fell into step beside her, "You saw me talking to Captain Morris?"

"I saw you talking to an officer. I didn't know his name. But I know he's captain of the King's Guard."

"And one of Sinifir's henchmen. Also the main instructor for the assassins. I'm glad you told me about the daggers. He was here asking me to return them."

They continued walking in the direction of the royal residences. "But you would think he knew where they were?"

"Apparently not. I'm going to confront Prince Stephen and demand their return. And I want to see your quarters."

Katrina raised an eyebrow. "My quarters? Why would you want to see..."

"We can't continue to meet in the palm garden. They – Sinifir and Prince Stephen, or one of their willing servants – will probably be keeping a closer watch over you from now on. Obviously, possession of the daggers has aroused their suspicions, no matter how innocent and plausible our accounting of it. So, lead on."

A few moments later they arrived. As she had previously described, her suite was at the end of the royal residence hall. The floors were covered in rugs of various size, color and shape. She paused before the next-to-last door. "These are Prince Stephen's quarters. What next?"

"I knock." He did. There was a muffled 'who's there... what do you want ... go away'. Marcus knocked again.

The door swung open. Prince Stephen had been sleeping, drinking, or both. His clothes were wrinkled, his hair in disarray, and he was clearly unshaven. He looked at Marcus. They were acquainted, having spent a handful of turns together in youth classes. "Marcus. What are you doing in the royal residences. And what do you want with me?"

'I believe you have something of mine. Two things actually." A bit of alarm came into Stephen's eyes. Marcus did a light mind-touch. *He knows I'm here about the daggers.*

Stephen lied, as expected. "Haven't a clue what you are talking about," He then tried to close the door.

Marcus placed his foot inside the room, stopping the door's closing. "Oh I think you know. Certainly so, if you take a moment to think about it. Daggers. The two I loaned to your sister for casting practice? She said you searched her room, without her permission, and took them from her. Well, they were mine to lend, not yours to take. I've been asked to return them, so please give them to me."

"Uh, well, I can't. I don't have them. I gave them to Captain Morris several days ago."

Marcus was quiet for a long moment. "Prince Stephen, I think not. It was Captain Morris that called on me this morning demanding their return. Want to try again, without lying this time?"

Prince Stephen glared at Marcus, then shoved him back into the hall and slammed the door.

Marcus turned to Katrina. "Can you summon someone from the castle staff? I want to see your rooms. But I would not do so without a proper escort."

Katrina disappeared into her quarters, returning a moment later. "My maid has been summoned. She shall be here in a... Oh, there she is now."

A matronly middle-aged woman approached, bowing to the princess. 'M'lady. You called?"

"Yes, Jocinda. This is Marcus, my second cousin and blades instructor. He wanted to see my casting station, but declined to enter my quarters without a proper escort." Katrina opened the door and waved them forward. "Would you please lead us in, and remain during his visit?'

"Yes,m'lady. Of course I'll stay." She gave Marcus an appraising eye, obviously pleased with his honorable conduct.

Katrina's quarters were nicely appointed. There was a small foyer followed by a sitting room. Doors led from there. She pointed to them. "Bedroom and closets are on the left, my toilet is to the right. It isn't much, but certainly adequate for my needs."

Marcus saw a large wooden shield affixed to the sitting room wall. Beneath it was a piles of rugs, covered with various small wood splinters. Before he could comment, Katrina's door burst open. Prince Stephen stumbled in, followed by several of the palace guard. "This man..." sputtered the Prince, "... this man is violating my sister's..."

Marcus completed the sentence. "Your sister's *honor?* I think not. Jocinda, perhaps you can explain your presence here?"

Jocinda was caught in an uncomfortable position, standing between two royals. She stammered a reply. "The man, who says he is both the princess's cousin and instructor, wished to see m'lady's quarters. But insisted I be present as an escort, should questions arise." She bowed respectfully. "M'Lord."

Stephen was in a scarlet rage. "Seen what you came to see?"

Marcus turned and in a blur of motion, drew a casting blade from his belt and flung it at the target. With a solid *thunk*, it buried itself deeply into the center heart of the shield. He followed the first with four more in rapid succession. Everyone but Katrina was struck dumb. Marcus turned back to Prince Stephen. "I am leaving these blades with Katrina. For her practice. I trust you will find no reason to take them from her? And I expect you to return the daggers to either me, or to Captain Morris. It is your choice. But I want them returned by tomorrow after last-meal." With that he swept from her room and strode down the hall, away from the royal quarters. He had accomplished his two tasks. First, confront Prince Stephen about the violation of Katrina's privacy and theft of daggers. And second, capture enough detail to reliable port to her quarters.

The next day Captain Morris visited Marcus shortly after the mid-day meal, before classes had resumed. "You need bother yourself no more regarding the daggers. They have been recovered, returned." With those terse words, he turned and left. No explanation expected, none given.

Marcus took note of a slight man, dressed in a faded tunic and long pants. He loitered about the training areas. It was uncommon for visitors to be present. His attention seemed to be focused on the students, Katrina in particular. To Marcus, the man's purpose was clear. He was there to constantly surveil the princess. Marcus, therefore, avoided any contact with her. This was an easy task, as she had become more assistant instructor than student, so had little need of his individual attention. It being a third-day, the post mid-day was devoted to short-blade work. Rather than practice in casting, Marcus instructed his trainees to return to the sparring arena. "There is another dimension to short-blade work, and that is close-in combat. Actually, if a confrontation comes down to this, consider yourself in a precarious situation. It is more akin to melee than blades-man ship. Combat involving short-blades is unpredictable, even for the most highly trained blades-men. We will begin with a few fundamentals, but only occasionally return to it for further training. I will need two volunteers. Josef ... and Katrina, I think. Stand half-pace apart, facing each other. Josef, that looks correct. Katrina, let me show you how to position your feet properly."

As he stood behind her, his head next to her, she whispered. "Talk. Tonight. Same time."

"Lock your door. I will port directly to your room."

That evening, Marcus told his father he would be going out for a short walk, explaining that the day's training had left him quite tense."

"Problems, Marcus?"

"No more than ordinary. But the last two seven-days have been stressful. Some quiet, alone time would be to my liking. Do you object?"

"Oh, of course not. But will you be leaving the castle grounds?"

"No. There are plenty of gardens and orchards here. I might just find a bench somewhere and sit awhile. Sit and put my mind to rest."

"Well, enjoy yourself. Any idea how long you will be gone?"

"It will not be late, back well before our normal bed time, I'm sure."

Marcus made his way to a very dark corner of a somewhat untended garden area. It was close on to one of the castle walls that blocked the sun for much of the post mid-day. When he was confident he was alone and un-followed, he ported to Katrina's room. When he arrived, it was clear she was glad to see him. It was equally clear she had been weeping.

Marcus waited until her sobbing subsided. "Stephen is terrible! He blames me for the embarrassment you heaped on him yesterday. He called me a *hofa. A HOFA!*"

Marcus was shocked. "A pig's mother? A hofa?"

"Yes, and you're a hofun."

"A pig's father. Well, for what it's worth. I've been called worse. And probably deservedly so. But Katrina, he had no reason to call you such. It's a reflection on him, not on you."

She wiped her eyes on the sleeve of her blouse. "Yes, I know. But it still hurts. There's more though, much more. Prince Stephen is furious with you. It's all he can talk about, pacing back and forth across his room. He gave Sinifir a full account of yesterday's confrontation. Distorted of course in his favor. And he is *demanding* that Sinifir makes you the next target of the assassins."

"And what has been Sinifir's reaction to that?"

"Well, he hasn't said much, except try to settle my brother down. Sinifir now knows who you really are, and told him your death would be too visible. But he promised 'when the time comes, he will be dealt with'. And Sinifir told Stephen to quit the drinking. He needed to be sober and clear-headed for what they have to do next."

"Any comments on Camden?"

"Yes, a lot. That's why they were so upset about the daggers. They thought somehow the ones I had were Camden's. They are apparently missing, along with his purse. And his boots." She wrinkled her brow. "Why boots?"

"Boots are an easy sale for a thief. Not everyone can afford them."

"They believe Camden's own clumsiness brought about his death. 'He was probably skulking about, made himself a ready target to a better man'. They don't suspect anyone in their circle of friends, or enemies."

"Good they think that. So, are they going to try again, on Abbott?"

"No, at least they didn't discuss anything more."

There was a knock on the door, its handle rattled as someone tried to enter. Karina answered. "Just a moment, I'll be right there." Marcus took the opportunity to port back to his quarters.

There was a note waiting for him the next evening. The threesome wanted to meet not on the next seventh-day, but tomorrow, the fifth. The location was again, different, and a bit more distant from the castle. It was in a more run-down part of Alexa.

There was also a note from Saul, indicating he would be late returning home owing to 'pressing matters with the King'. Marcus added a brief note below his. *Retiring early, please do not disturb.* With that he went to his room. As before, he arranged pillows to give an appearance that he was abed and asleep. He changed into dark and inconspicuous clothing, donned his short-blades, and ported to the abandoned garden he had used previously. He quietly made his way from there, through the west gate, then on to the tavern where his friends were waiting.

Greta: "I guess you heard about Camden. Murdered and robbed."

Marcus: "Yes, I did. How are the trainees taking it? Anyone upset?"

"Ivan: "Upset? No. No one liked him that much. And will miss him even less. But it certainly sobered everyone up. Training has been really intense this seven-day. We all know it's a deadly business we're getting into. But there's always been the thought that we'd be the hunters, rather than the hunted."

Greta: "You wouldn't know anything about his... death?"

Marcus. "No comment."

Thomas grunted. "We thought so. Your sec'rets safe wid us."

Marcus: "No more talk about the next 'assignment' he's going to give out?"

Greta: "I think losing Camden has made him cautious. Hence, more training required."

Ivan: "Which is good as we don't need to make a decision yet, to stay or go."

Marcus: "I think that door has closed already. You know too much for him to simply let you walk away. So, be cautious."

The three looked at him with alarm.

Thomas: "Hadn't thought of it that way. I think yer right, Marcus. Goin' to be hard gettin' out."

With that, the meeting ended and they took their separate ways home.

Katrina was absent the following day. And the next. And again, the next. Fearing she might be ill, Marcus ported to her quarters the evening of the third day. He found her sitting sadly in her parlor.

"Oh Marcus, I knew you would come!"

"You have missed training. Are you ill?"

She began to sob. "No, I am well. But Stephen has locked me in, made me a prisoner in my own rooms. I'm not allowed to leave. And no visitors, not even Jocinda. They bring me food. They clear my bed-pans. Otherwise, I'm alone. Something is afoot, Marcus, and they clearly want me out of the way."

"They are still angry about the episode with the daggers?"

"Oh, for sure. But there appears to be more happening that just that. Sinifir is speaking less to Prince Stephen. I think my brother has become something of a problem, given his recent instabilities. Since Sinifir seems reluctant to move against you, Stephen has decided to move against me."

"I see. It might take several days, but let me work getting you out of here. But you are safe?"

"Yes, I'm safe. At least for now. I'm inconvenienced, for sure. But not threatened in any other particular way."

"Perhaps. But sooner or later your absence will be noticed by more than me. At which time Prince Stephen will be hard pressed for an explanation. My guess is that Sinifir knows nothing of your imprisonment. I think Stephen is headed for a great fall from grace, with him and everyone else. But you're safe, that's the important thing for now." With that Marcus ported back to his bedroom.

The next morning Marcus intercepted his grandfather as he was leaving their quarters. It was early. "Grandfather, I need a favor."

"Yes, my son. What would it be? You know I'm always happy to help." He paused. "If I am able."

"Well, in this instance, I am quite sure you can. It's about Katrina, Crown Prince Jared's daughter."

"She is unwell?"

"That's just it. I don't know. She seemed well last sixth-day, in our training class. But she has been absent the last three. There is a rumor circulating, that she is being detained in her quarters. Against her will. Perhaps you could mention it to her father and have it investigated? And by the way, she has been constantly surveilled the last several seven-days. It is obvious to everyone, and it has been unsettling to the class. It has only ended during her absence."

"Of course, son. I would be happy to mention it to the Crown

Prince. In fact, I am leaving now for a meeting in which he will be present."

It was late when Marcus felt he could port away without arousing suspicion from his grandfather. He arrived to find Katrina in high spirits.

"Oh, Marcus! You should have been here this post mid-day! It was great! My father came asking if I were well, and was challenged by the sentry standing outside my door. 'Why are you posted here outside my daughter's door?' He told my father I was being detained 'for my own safety, and at the command of Prince Stephen'. My father lost no time making it clear I was to be released. Immediately. The guard, if you can believe this, actually refused! He refused a direct order by the Crown Prince! The palace guard that had accompanied my father took him into custody. Where he is now I do not know. Not in a good place, I am sure. Anyway, when my father entered and asked, I told him the simple truth. Prince Stephen had ordered someone to follow me for the last two seven-days. And for the last three days he had confined me, by force, to my room. Father stormed out, returning a moment later with my brother in tow. When asked why he ordered me confined, Stephen gave some feeble excuse about 'for my protection'. When my father asked *me* if I thought I needed protection, I pointed at my brother and said, 'only from him and his evil friend Sinifir'."

"You actually implicated Sinifir?"

"Yes, well, it kind of slipped out. But it's no secret that the two of them are close. And up to great mischief."

"What about the surveillance? Did he mention that?"

"Yes, my father did. He said 'and make the surveillance of your sister stop. Now'. But the best part is yet to come! My father confined Stephen to *his* room and posted a guard with instructions to let Stephen summon a messenger to end my surveillance. Thereafter, no one was to visit unless he *personally* authorized otherwise. Let's see how Stephen likes being treated the way he treated me!"

Marcus laughed. "Looks like you will be in class tomorrow, then?"

"I should be. Oh, and thanks for helping me get released. I know you got word to my father, somehow."

"You're welcome. What else are cousins good for, right?" And with that, he ported back to his bedroom.

The next morning she was in class, happy, and without surveillance.

His grandfather was late in arriving home. He was in high spirits. "We've received a message by a fast-rider. The envoy from Caldonia has reached Sudsport. He will be here within a seven-day."

"And that is *good* news?" asked Marcus.

His grandfather's enthusiasm faded. "*Fata* alone knows." He then brightened up. "But at least it's a step in the right direction. If the envoy makes it clear to the King that no hostilities exist, or have existed, it might get him to back away from these military preparations. And expenses! By the *fata*, the cost will be ruinous if it continues much longer."

"So you are convinced the envoy's influence with the King will be enough to offset Sinifir's?"

"Yes. Well, let's hope so. I don't know how the King can decide otherwise."

Marcus was thinking furiously. *So my grandfather and Crown Prince Jared are under-estimating Sinifir once again. Are they falling under his influence, in spite of their precautions? It looks to me as if they are. Sinifir's strategy is clear. The envoy preaches peace but assassinates a royal. And what better royal that the Crown Prince, who just happens to be leading the army? Everything would turn Sinifir's way. The King declares war, Sinifir is given charge of the military. And on it goes. The assassins secretly eliminate any who oppose.*

"Grandfather, we all know Sinifir cannot be trusted. I would be very careful, He is a devious man and plans many moves ahead. You and the Crown Prince need to take special precautions for your lives. Your assassination, or his, or the assassination of you both? With blame placed on the envoy? It would give Sinifir everything he wants."

Saul thought for a few moments. "You are right. But do you really think Sinifir would go that far? Actually use assassinations to achieve his ends?"

"Yes, grandfather, I have no doubts whatsoever. Why else would he have recruited them?"

"I will discuss this with the Crown Prince. In the meantime, there are many things to prepare. How are you at dancing?"

"Dancing? Why would you ask about dancing at a time like this?"

"Because the King has decided we should fete the Caldonian envoy with a feast, followed by a royal ball."

"We actually do that?"

"Why, yes my dear boy. It's been a while, I grant you. The last when the Crown Prince wed. That would have been some turns before you were born. In any case, as part of the extended royal household, we will be attending. And you will be expected to dance with the young ladies. Won't that be fun!"

Marcus thought back to his lessons in dance, as a child. Everyone was required to master traditional reels and folk dances containing a complicated series of steps. It had been fun to learn back then. But would be difficult to remember now. "Grandfather, that was many turns ago. And I've never danced since. I'm unlikely to make a good impression if I try."

"Nonsense, my boy. Besides, you will have a seven-day to practice. *As the King commands!*"

"But, what about my training classes?"

"Oh, don't worry. Kelson will find a way to cover them. Or maybe not, if the trainees become part of the dance troupe. Let them know you'll be otherwise engaged, starting tomorrow. You will need to be ready a seven-day from this seventh. Let this be the end of it. *As the King commands!*"

"Yes," groaned Marcus. "*As the King commands.*"

The royal musicians were rarely called on to perform. The stringed instruments were adequately represented. The horn section less so. Drummers and cymbalists were drawn from the military marching corps. The first two days of dance were somewhat unproductive, as the musicians slowly sorted themselves into some form of rhythm and tune. Katrina, of course, was a member of the troupe. Unfortunately, the dances to be performed were group oriented. There would be no close-dancing, much to Marcus' (and Katrina's?) disappointment.

By the fifth-day, Marcus was feeling better about the upcoming ball. The moves and patterns he had learned as a child were quick to return. Katrina was several turns younger, and therefore, that many turns closer to her dance training.

CHAPTER
FOURTEEN

Marcus took a casual walk through the training areas. He was not surprised to find a note from his three friends in its usual hiding place. It requested an urgent meet for third-day, this very night. As usual, he memorized the location and destroyed the small parchment on which the note had been written. He ported to a known location near his destination and made his way to the inn. His friends were tucked into a dark corner, waiting. Greta was the group's voice.

"Well, we have received our assignments. We are all going to the banquet and ball this coming seventh, which is what, four days from tonight? We will all be dressed as servants and kitchen staff. Matthew will be the main assassin. His target will be the crown prince and your grandfather. Unfortunately, we don't know the details. Our jobs will be to make sure he succeeds. In the chaos, we are to dispatch any of the King's guards who interfere with his escape. Captain Morris is hoping he and we will be unsuspected and we will all simply walk away."

"So what have you decided to do, or not do?"

Greta looked at the others. They all nodded. "We will be

attending as ordered, but will provide no assistance of any kind. We are pretty sure this is but the first two of many more assassinations to follow. Captain Morris has hinted at many 'enemies of the King' that must be dealt with."

Marcus let out a sigh. "Well, they will have us *dancing* as part of the after-dinner entertainment. I'll be keeping my eyes open and can hopefully prevent it from happening. I will make sure my grandfather and the Crown Prince know they are at risk."

There wasn't much more to discuss, so they ended the meeting and left their separate ways. Marcus found a dark alley and ported directly to his room.

Saul: "The King has made another request. And it involves you personally."

Marcus: "I'm afraid to ask. What will it be this time?"

Saul: "He wants you to perform a blade-dance, with real blades, of course. Somehow, he remembers seeing you blade-dance when you were young, and thought it would make a sure impression on the Caldonian envoy. You will have to get a couple of long-blades from the armory and start practicing. I've seen you dance the blades, and it really is quite a spectacle."

Blade dancing was something all blades-men practiced. It was a constant form of entertainment, from trainees to blade-masters. Marcus had become very good, not just with one blade, but with a blade in each hand. But he did not want to be distracted in such a way, when so much depended on his constant surveillance and the protection of his grandfather and the Crown Prince.

"Grandfather, there is an alternative, you know. Katrina, the King's own granddaughter, is every bit as good as I am. And much better to look at. Why don't you suggest this to the King."

"Well, I guess I can. I'll ask and let you know tomorrow. In the meantime, you should practice in case he says 'no'."

The dancers, Marcus included, were in a frolicking folk dance when Saul entered the castle ballroom to observe. When they broke for a brief rest, he sought out both Marcus and Katrina. "Marcus, have you spoken to Katrina about the request I make last night?"

Marcus shook his head.

Saul turned to Katrina. "Your grandfather, the King, has asked for Marcus to perform a blade-dance as part of the after-dinner entertainment. Marcus thought that you, as the King's granddaughter, might be a better choice."

Katrina shot Marcus a scornful glance.

"Well, I discussed it with the King, and I think he thought it was a good idea, that is, until Sinifir got involved. He persuaded the King that 'two blade-dancers might be even more impressive. And since I would be standing with the King, each of us would have a grandchild on display'. The King thought this was a marvelous idea. Or perhaps Sinifir persuaded him to think it would be. So there it is. You will both be blade-dancing immediately after all of this concludes." Saul stretched out his hands in the direction of the other dancers. "Not that I like it much, either. But, *as the King commands*." And with that, he turned his back to them and left the ballroom.

"Oh great! Thanks, cousin. I don't need enemies when I have friends like you."

They walked off to an empty corner of the ballroom. Marcus whispered. "The word from my friends is that there will be an assassination attempt on your father and my grandfather. I wanted to be free to observe. And if necessary, to act. I think Sinifir knows that, and is trying to keep me distracted. It's the only thing that makes sense. Think about it, a *blade-dance*. I don't know about you, but I haven't really practiced blade-dancing for several turns. I remember seeing you, though, showing off to the other trainees. You really are good, I mean, *really* good. I, not so much."

Katrina let out a sound somewhere between a sigh and a groan.

"Well, it isn't like we can get out of it in any possible way. How do you propose we do it? One blade or two?"

"I would prefer two, if that's acceptable with you. But they will have to be real. I don't want to be defending our fathers armed with wooden blades, when the assassins are using steel. So we should probably go to the armory when this class ends, and find blades to our liking. I know we need some intense practice in the next two days."

They caught the arms-master just as he was locking up and leaving for his evening meal. "Sir, could you spare us a few moments, please."

"Of course, Marcus, and ...?"

"Katrina, sir. One of his trainees."

"Yes, of course, I've seen you around from time to time. Your long-blade work is quite good. And I'm also impressed with your short-blade casting. Are you still working with the blades Marcus checked out for your practice?"

"Yes, and thank you. I need to be returning them to you. I've had them for a long time, now."

'Oh, nothing to worry about. I know where they are and I have plenty more. Now, what can I do for you?"

"Have you heard about the banquet and ball planned for the coming seventh?"

"Yes, heard rumors. Captain Morris checked out some extra weapons for the King's guards."

Marcus' blood ran chill. "Well, Katrina and I have been asked by the King to entertain his guests with a blade-dance. We each need a pair of real blades. Could we look over what's available, and maybe find some that would serve our purpose?"

"Why, of course. Come in and let me show you what I have."

The armory held a vast array of weapons. Katrina asked for a suggestion. "This will be before the King and his guests, so we want something that looks respectable."

"Well, yes, that's certain. I actually have some shiny new blades that have just arrived for military officers. Let's look through those."

A short time later Marcus and Katrina departed, each carrying sheathed long-blades. Katrina's were a bit shorter and lighter than those Marcus had chosen. Blade-dancing was anciently performed with curved, thick-bellied long-blades, called sabers. Those had long-ago given way to t traditional long-blades. Marcus had selected a pair similar to Katrina's, with ornate quillons and knuckle guards. All four long-blades were formidable weapons.

"And now we practice. Tomorrow we will have to practice *together*, and select some music for our dance. Do you want to do it before or after the regular dance practice?"

"Or during practice, at mid-day? Either before or after the break for mid-day meal?" suggested Katrina.

"How about immediately after. It would give the other dancers a bit of entertainment."

Marcus and Katrina stood a pace apart. The orchestra began a waltz and blades began to move, slowly at first, then at an increasing tempo. The moves were those of *tai kai*, all four-hand two positions flowing from one to the next, repeated. They were both excellent blade-men. The other dancers stood in a large circle, mesmerized by the flashing weapons. The blades twisted and turned in their intricate patterns, always faster. They adjusted their moves to be exact duplicates. They were, after all, patterns they practiced daily. After a while they called it to a halt. There would be time for more practice the next two days.

On sixth day, the last day of dance training, Marcus came home to find a guest in their quarters. An old high-mage, identified by a dark robe with gilded trim, sat across the small table from his grandfather. They each had a tankard of ale at hand. "This is my grandson, of whom we have been talking. Marcus, Lord High-mage Bartholomew of Caldonia."

Marcus bowed in respect. "An honor to meet you, sir."

The old mage nodded in return and turned to Saul. "And polite, too. You have done a good job with him, my friend. I've wondered how it would turn out, losing Bekka and all."

Marcus spoke, even though it was impolite to do so until spoken to. "You know each other, or knew each other before now?"

Saul gave Marcus a look of disappointment. "Well, yes. This is not the first time Bartholomew has braved the Betting Sea to visit our blessed Isle. But it has been many, many turns ago, long before you were born. We have corresponded in the turns since, from time to time. You will find, Marcus, that the mage community is loosely connected where ever you go."

Bartholomew: "Which is why I have come as companion to the Caldonian envoy, Prince William. Who, by the way, is the King's brother. We were much concerned with Iber's request for a conference." He turned to Saul. "Especially after I received your letter concerning our common foe, Sinifir."

"Excuse me, sir, for asking. But you, in Caldonia, know of Sinifir?"

"Oh yes, he passed through some turns ago. He tried to ingratiate himself with our King. Unfortunately for him, our King is *gifted* and quickly perceived his meddling. We promptly banished him from Caldonia. We didn't realize he had dared the Betting Sea to come here."

Saul addressed Marcus. "There are those who suspect your involvement in all of this. It increases the likelihood of an assassination attempt on you, as well as on the Crown Prince and myself. Precautions are being taken. But the reason Bartholomew is here is not about tomorrow's events, but about *you*."

"About *me*, grandfather?"

"Yes, about you. Bartolomew, you will explain?"

"Marcus, your grandfather has told me about your experiences with *gift*. We agree that you are powerfully endowed. This is good, as *gift* is always welcomed, especially in the royal courts. But it is also *bad* in that it can lead the bearer into dangerous avenues. Sinifir being a case in point."

"But I would never..."

"...Never what? Become evil and twisted like Sinifir? If you believe that, you do *not* understand how strongly *gift-power* can seduce. It is why the academy at Holtsclaw Abbey was established, many, many turns ago."

Marcus shot a look at his grandfather. "Holtsclaw Abbey? Where is that? You know this place?"

Saul nodded. "Know of it, yes. Know it personally, no. It is an academy reserved for those who have already demonstrated *gift*. And due to its cost, those who attend are either royal or from the wealthiest of families."

Bartholomew: "It's a four-turn program, dedicated to understanding the history of *gift*, refining and expanding *gift* skills, and learning the precautions that should be followed in its use. It also focuses on physical fitness, decorum -- manners, if you will – and self protection. Interns – that's what they are called, mage-interns – come to the school about your age, or a turn or two older. It's an austere program, very intense. Strict discipline is maintained. Those who complete the four turns will leave bearing the title of *mage*. And will be fully capable of defending themselves with blade, bow and *gift*. Your grandfather has said you are already accomplished with both blades and ranged weapons?"

"Yes. I am currently instructing the youngest trainees with blades."

"Well, so much the advantage for you, then."

Marcus gave the old mage a puzzled look. "For me? Are you suggesting I should go to this academy?"

"No, not suggesting. Insisting. And your grandfather agrees."

"If I go, when would I need to leave? If I actually go that is. But you said it is very expensive."

"You will need to leave early in the second turning. Each turn at the academy begins at the beginning of the fourth turning and lasts three. Getting there from here will be a problem, as will the cost. Holtsclaw Abbey lies on the eastern-most territory of Tumano, not far from its frontier with Adnium. Even from Caldonia it's more than hand-fist leagues. It will be a hard trip and long. So it's unlikely you will return until the four turns have passed. Now, as for the cost. Saul will have to consult with the King on that. Tuition, which includes both room and board, of course, has been the same for living memory. One gold crown per turning, three crowns per turn. It could be greater for you, four crowns per turn, since you would not be returning here for the third turning, but remaining at the Abbey."

"One gold... per *turning*? That's, that's *outrageous!*" exclaimed Marcus. "If I have to stay there the full turn, for four turns, that would be *a hand six crowns*. That's... that's a fortune. Iber doesn't even have that kind of coin, does it, grandfather?"

Saul nodded his head several times. "Yes, Marcus, it is a great sum. And yes, Iber has that kind of coin. Though the King is loathe to spend it. Actually, he is spending much more than that to maintain this silly army of Sinifir's. And that's just one more reason to have this whole affair with Sinifir come to an end. If he continues funding an army, he will exhaust the King's treasury."

Bartholomew resumed speaking. "Well, problems for you to solve, I'm afraid. Not much for me to do with it. But there is one thing I can do, which is to write you a letter of introduction to the Lord-mage of Holtsclaw, Petros. We were class-mates there, many, many turns ago."

There were a few more polite words spoken, then Bartholomew took his leave.

Well, grandfather, we have a short night and a long day ahead of us." I wonder how much our world will have changed by this time tomorrow night."

Saul said nothing, simply nodded in agreement.

———

There was to be a final practice that morning, what the instructors called a *dress rehearsal*. Marcus arrived to find several tables full of ornate, traditional, outfits for the dancers. He found the one with his name pinned to the vest. They appeared to be his size. Marcus was not pleased. The pants were tight-fitting and the vest restricted his movements. The billowing sleeves would surely interfere with blade-dancing. Nevertheless, wear them he was required to do. Privacy screens had been set up for changing. When all were properly attired, it made for a colorful troupe. At mid-day the instructors pronounced them *ready*. They were dismissed and told to report back before the banquet. Well, all except Marcus and Katrina. They were to have one more session with blade-dancing. Thankfully, it was to be after the mid-day meal rather than before.

They sat in a quiet corner of the common eating area for castle staff. "My father came and spoke to Stephen this morning. He has had him constantly guarded, secluded and distant from Sinifir. But he has granted him leave to attend today's festivities. As he said, it would not look good to have his own heir missing. But he warned Stephen to be on good behavior. And to stay far away from Sinifir. After he left, Stephen went into another total rage, cursing our father and swearing to 'have his head' for this humiliation. And somehow he has me mixed up in it. He swore my death as well, but not until he had properly 'used' me. I'm sure you know what that means. Marcus, I am terrified for the future. If he were ever to ascend to the throne, the *fata* forbid, there's no telling what trouble he would create. And his resentment against me is unlikely to change over time."

Marcus nodded in agreement. "Then you haven't heard anything more about the assassination attempt?"

"No. It's unlikely, given that the two of them have not been able to meet. Now that there's no guard at the door, it's possible Sinifir will try to bring Stephen up to date. After we practice, I'm going back to my room to listen. Hopefully I'll hear something useful."

"Well, then, let's get this practice behind us. There are a few things I need to do as well."

The costume, as Marcus feared, made blade-dancing more difficult. It took concentration to keep the whirling blades free from the billowing sleeves. Those same sleeves, however, might let him conceal a fore-arm sheath with several casting blades? He would have to undress and redress discretely to avoid their detection by the other dancers. Security would be tight. Blades were sure to be reported if seen.

Upon returning home, Marcus found his grandfather sitting again with Bartholomew. The old mage gave Marcus a letter, securely closed with an ornate red wax seal. "Your letter of introduction to Holtsclaw. I trust you can keep it dry and safe?"

"Of course, sir, and thank you. How I am to get there, and with the proper coin? Well, that remains a mystery."

"Yes, things to work out," said Saul. "But I believe they will. It will take a full two turnings to make the journey afoot, so we have what, more than a full turning to prepare for it? Which brings up another matter for you, Bartholomew."

"Which is...?"

"Your return to Caldonia. We're well into the third turning, heading all too soon into the storms of the fourth. You need to hasten your return across the Betting Sea."

"Yes, I have discussed it with the Envoy. We are planning on leaving next second-day. Give us a day of recovery from tonight's gala, and we will be on our way."

"So you think you have accomplished what you came here to do?"

"Quite frankly, we don't know. We have made it as clear as we can that we have no hostilities toward Iber. Nor do we intend any. Baring any untoward actions tonight, we leave as we came, at peace. But with Sinifir constantly tickling the King's ear, it might not be enough. We have long had a resident *friend* here in Alexa to keep us posted on your affairs. He has been reminded to be especially vigilant. For all concerned, I think it best if his name be left unsaid, even here."

"Agreed," said Saul. "Will I see you sometime on first-day? And surely I shall be there for your departure on the following." The two men shook hands and Bartholomew left.

"Well, Marcus, the banquet starts shortly. But I think I will take a short nap. It promises to be a long evening and one with plenty of drink. And the drink? It doesn't appeal to me as much as it once might have. I have no objection if you choose to partake. But you will need to do it in moderation. When one is not accustomed to it, it takes but little to affect one's well-being and judgment. And it just might be that tonight we will have need of *all* your faculties, both physical and mental. And before you say anything more, I know you have *mind-gift*. That's what brought your *gift* to the attention of Kelson turns ago. Now go! I need my sleep."

Marcus hurried to the armory, finding the arms-master in his office bent over a parchment.

"Marcus, my man! What can I do for you today? I thought you would be up to your chin in preparations for the big gala and your blade-dance. You realize, of course, that everyone is talking about them, especially your blade-dancing with that young lady... Katrina? Wasn't that her name? I didn't know she was a Princess, Crown Prince Jared's daughter and all. Anyway, as I said, your blade-dancing has been the talk of all the blades-men, especially those in the King's guard. Wish I could be there to see it! But then, not much hope that a nobody such as I would be invited to such a fancy affair."

"Don't put yourself down, sir. You are a good man in an

important position. And for what it's worth, I would *gladly* change places with you. But... that's not going to happen, I fear."

"No, not likely at all," the arms-master said with a chuckle. "Now, I know you be coming here for some reason or another. What do you need *this* time?"

"You are so suspicious! Always thinking I need something! Well, of course, you are right as usual. I need three or four casting blades and a neck-sheath to hide them. I thought about a wrist-sheath, but the sleeves are tight around my lower arms and I wouldn't have ready access."

"Casting blades? So you are expecting trouble," the arms-master said sadly. "I've been worried about that, with assassins being trained up and all. I have never liked that Captain Morris, even less so as of late .Some of those boys of his are just no good. Live long enough, you can tell. You are good to be free of him."

"So you've guessed what he's about. I guess that's not so hard. Given their work with daggers and such."

"Yes. I know weapons. The dagger has always been an assassin's blade. Captain Morris had me hold all of 'em till he had need. There's still eight pairs of them unaccounted for, so be alert tonight. Here, let's go see what I can do for you with the casting blades you want."

Marcus left somewhat later with a sheath that strapped over each shoulder and buckled in the back. It held three casting blades. He found he could reach behind his neck, retrieve, and cast a blade in one quick motion. He spent a brief time in practice and left satisfied. The arms-master grasped him by the forearms as he left. "I trust you to keep the King safe. Promise me you will do whatever you need to do to keep him safe. These Caldonians, I don't know. Rumors are they are a peaceful lot. But you never truly know, do yuh?"

"I will do my best, sir. And thank you for your help." Marcus returned to his quarters.

CHAPTER
FIFTEEN

I t was a great honor to be invited to the King's royal banquet and ball. The noble family itself was not large. Even counting distant cousins it amounted to less than two-hand adult men and women. The remaining seven-hand who were attending represented the wealthy, what his grandfather called the *community of coin*. And senior military officers. The banquet tables were arranged around the grand ballroom, leaving the middle open for the after-meal performances. The King and his family sat at the head table. Crown Prince Jared sat next to the King, then Stephen and Katrina. To the King's left sat the Caldonian Envoy, Prince William, then Bartholomew, Lord-high Mage Saul and Marcus. Sinifir, obviously annoyed he was not seated at the head table, sat with other dignitaries at an adjacent table. It was a pace away and a full step lower. Everyone was dressed in their finery. Marcus and Katrina were the exceptions, wearing costumes reflecting their eventual performances. There were guards-men posted in various places, always several within three or four paces of the King. Royal banners had been hung from the walls. An especially beautiful one, depicting an ancient scene of horsemen contending with a great forest bear, had been hung over the dark wooden paneling directly behind the royal table. The banquet tables were covered in perfectly pressed, white rope-weed cloth. The dishes and plates were adorned with gilded edges. And the table ware, at least at the head table, were of silver with inlaid gold filigree. The royal musicians played a quiet waltz while the guests were escorted to their assigned seats. At a signal, the orchestra drew its music to a close. Guests arose, and in the respectful silence that followed, the final four entered and were seated: the King, followed by the Caldonian Envoy Prince William, Crown Prince Jared and Lord High-mage Bartholomew. When they sat, the others did also. A few moments later, the King stood again and addressed those attending.

"Please all arise. Family and friends of Iber. As your King, it has been my pleasure to host these who sit beside me. We have met in the spirit of peace and reconciliation. I am pleased to announce that any prior misunderstandings have been resolved. We look forward to continuing our long-standing peaceful relationship. I am sure you all join with me in wishing them a quick and safe return to Caldonia. And that the Betting Sea deals with them kindly." A murmur of soft laughter passed through the room. "So now I propose a toast." He held his wine goblet to arms-length and high, "To our neighboring Kingdom, Caldonia and those here among us who represent her and her King. A toast of continuing peace between them and our own Kingdom of Iber. *To Iber and Caledonia!*"

To Iber and Caldonia echoed loudly throughout the Ballroom. Sips were taken, and all returned to their seats.

The food was served, first to the head table (beginning, of course, with the King), then to the others. The kitchen staff was smartly dressed in clean and pressed uniforms. They distributed food in quick, practiced motions. The first course was soup, a delicious light broth with a seafood base. This was cleared and salads were offered, a choice between greens festooned with colorful vegetables, or an elaborate arrangement of fresh fruit. The main course also provided choice: roast venison, grilled fish, or fowl stuffed with a heavily spiced breading.

After a lengthy time of eating and conversation, the dinner dishes were cleared away. The King again stood to address the attendees. "I understand that a delicious desert of fruit and finely whipped cream has been prepared." He turned to the Envoy. "And following that, as a final toast, our gracious guests from Caldonia have presented us with a cask of that spiced wine for which Caldonia is so renowned. While we will be enjoying this last part of the meal, the royal family has prepared for your enjoyment a medley of traditional dances." He turned to one of the ballroom alcoves where the dancers had been seated and served. "Music, please! And *dance!*"

Marcus and Katrina, sitting at opposite ends of the royal table, arose to join the other dancers. The musicians began to play, the dancers to dance. In spite of the short time they had to practice, the dances came off without much difficulty. There were a few miss-steps, for sure. But for the most part, every dancer performed well. At the end, the guests joined the King and the Envoy in a sincere and enthusiastic round of applause. The dancers returned to their alcove, Katrina and Marcus to the head table.

The King arose again. "As a special treat, we – I and my Lord High-mage, Saul Aurelius – have invited our respective grandchildren..." he pointed to his right... "Katrina, and..." pointing to his left "Marcus, to further entertainment with the exotic and beautiful blade-dance. Children, if you please."

Marcus and Katrina touched blades and retreated a step. They mirrored each other's movements. Blades slowly gyrated in an intricate figure-of-eight pattern, according to the flowing forms of *tai kai*. The blades passed in front, to the sides, and even behind their backs. They touched briefly from time to time with a clash of metal against metal. The tempo gradually increased. Marcus grew increasingly aware of her battle-mage *gift*. Without it, she would not have reached the speed at which they were now dancing. He felt her begin to tire. The blades were man-sized weapons. So he gently pushed her a trickle of *gift*. It had its desired effect. She regained her strength and further increased her tempo.

With a shock, Marcus realized he had completely forgotten about the possibility of an assassination attempt. He mentally touched Katrina's mind with the instruction to pause their routine on the count of three. *One – two – three.* They each took a step back, breaking their dance. Katrina's back was to the head table, giving Marcus a clear view of the unfolding events there. Matthew, all smiles and pleasantries and white uniform, was pouring wine into the goblet of the Crown Prince. He had surely served the King first. In his other hand Matthew held, half hidden, a small grey flask. He had no doubt the Envoy, Bartholomew and his grandfather would be served next.

With a great shout Marcus yelled "DO NOT DRINK – THE WINE HAS BEEN POISONED! THIS MAN IS AN ASSASSIN!" He hurled the long-blade, casting and guiding it with the influence of *gift*. Long-blades were not designed for casting. They were a slashing weapon. But Marcus cast one of his weapon with such velocity it passed easily through Matthew's arm and the tapestry behind the table, then embedded itself deeply in the wooden panel behind. Those seated at the table threw themselves to the floor in panic. Guardsmen rushed forward, surrounding Matthew, who was helplessly pinned to the wall. There was blood flowing freely from his impaled arm. Marcus took a quick look around the room. Four other assassins were serving wine: Ejay, Winston, Lindon and Carlos. As soon as they saw recognition in Marcus' eyes, each dropped his wine pitcher, drew a dagger, and seized a hostage. Marcus did not hesitate. In a single, quick motion, he drew a casting blade and sent it with unerring accuracy into Lindon's right eye. He followed with blades to Ejay and Winston.

This left only Carlos, at a far table, standing quite alone with his hostage. There was a soft *twang* and Carlos collapsed, a bolt squarely embedded in his forehead. A kings-guard stood some three or four paces away. He held a cross-bow on his shoulder and a satisfied smile on his lips.

Marcus nodded to him. "Marcus."

The guards-man nodded in return. "Marsdon."

"Thank you, Marsdon. I obviously needed one more blade."

Matthew, surrounded by guards-men, was contending his innocence. Marcus walked up to him and spoke calmly: "Easy enough to verify." He reached into Matthew's serving jacket and retrieved the small grey flask. He opened it and poured several drops into the Crown Prince's goblet. "Here, drink this!"

Matthew's face took on a look of horror. "No! No! I will tell everything. I was made to do this. The person responsible is..." A dazed look came upon his face. He snatched the small flask from Marcus' hand, brought it to his lips, and sucked in its contents. Whatever was inside brought him out of his trance. He looked at the flask, looked at Marcus, and started to speak. "I should have known he could not be trust..." His eyes rolled back into his head, he gasped, and fell instantly dead.

Everything had passed in but a few moments. Katrina still stood on the ballroom floor, long-blades in hand. Screams had barely subsided. The seven who had been sitting at the royal table began arising from the floor. One of the first was High-mage Bartholomew. "Let me see that flask!" he demanded. A guardsman retrieved it carefully from the floor where it had fallen and handed it to him. Bartholomew held it to his nose. "Dorlock. A powerful poison. Quick acting. Had you not intervened, Marcus, we would now be dead, or soon to be. How did you know?"

"These men are known to me. I trained with them briefly under Captain Morris, head of the King's guard. I quit when I suspected their training was to this very end."

An officer of the guard was standing next to the Crown Prince, who had joined their small group. "Captain Morris? Are you sure? And are there others? We need to clean out this... this nest of vipers."

"Yes, there are four more, and Captain Morris, who probably now lies dead. Of the four, only one is of concern. He is a big man, cruel, goes by the name of Louton. The other three are not assassins, but kept themselves involved in an attempt to prevent what was planned to happen here tonight. Make sure your men know this. Their names are Ivan, Greta and Thomas."

The officer acknowledged with a nod, turned to the other guardsmen standing by, and began issuing orders.

Marcus looked over to the table where Sinifir had been sitting. He was not there, though he had been moments before. *Nor was he anywhere to be seen. Ivan. Greta. Thomas. What have I just done? Sinifir would have heard what I told the guardsmen. And surely he will have you slain for your treachery.* Marcus looked over to the end of the royal table. Stephen, also, was missing.

It took some time to sort things out, but eventually guests were released to return home, as well as the performers and musicians. There were questions to be answered. particularly how the assassins were assigned to serve the final toast. That, at least, was quickly resolved. Captain Morris, head of the kings-guard, had insisted on their assignment as a special precaution for the King's *safety.* Out-ranked, the King's steward had obliged. It also became known that Captain Morris had intervened on the seating arrangements. The four tables being served by the assassins were assigned to the King's extended family and certain wealthy couples with known royal allegiances. It was no surprise to Marcus that Abbott and his wife were among them. It was obvious to Marcus and the royal family that the intent was not just to foment war. It was also intended to eliminate all direct and indirect claims to the throne. Sinifir's hand in these matters was not openly discussed, as he still held sway with the King.

At last, the only three remaining in the ballroom, except for the castle and kitchen staff busily cleaning and clearing, were Bartholomew, Saul and Marcus. "What to do, what to do? Doesn't this leave things a royal mess!" said Saul, in a voice of despair.

Mage Bartholomew harrumphed. "Could be a lot worse, my friend. You live, thanks to your grandson!"

"Grandfather, it might not be as bleak as you imagine. First, the assassination attempts failed. And as Lord Bartholomew just said, the team of assassins has been eliminated, or nearly so. The Envoy and you, Lord Bartholomew, can return to Caldonia with your mission accomplished. We still have to deal with Sinifir. But there are now many who are convinced of his role in these matters. And finally, there is at least one royal whom we can rely on to defend Iber and its royal family."

It took a few moments for the two high-mages to digest what Marcus had said. Saul was the first to speak. "You say there is a royal capable of defending Iber?"

"Yes. Katrina. She has emerged, as a battle-mage no less. Not strong, yet, but she will grow swiftly. Especially if there are competent teachers to guide her instruction. "

Bartholomew spoke: "I suspected as much. The blade-dance you performed was beyond skill and I sensed it was propelled by *gift*. Does that mean that you, Marcus, are also a battle-mage? I have thought you are either a mind-mage or an earth-mage, given what Saul has told me. So what exactly are you?"

Marcus was embarrassed, at a loss for words. "I... I guess I don't really know what I am. *Gift* comes easily, that's all that I can really say. I am beginning to believe my primary endowment might be as a battle-mage, even though there's no history of it in our line. Mind-mage as a secondary endowment is entirely possible."

"You know what he is, Bartholomew, as well as I do. And he

knows it too. He is, or will soon will be, a *master-mage*. And by solemn oath, we have an obligation to perform."

Bartholomew paled. "Yes, an oath we swore, with never an expectation to act upon it. As a mage, as a *high-mage* no less, I am loath to break any oath I make. But this one, this one I cannot abide." He turned to Marcus. "I'm sure this makes you uncomfortable. We here are talking about our obligation to take your life."

Marcus waved his hand. "Grandfather and I have had this discussion already. You speak of something of which I am fully aware. He has suggested alternatives, one of which is to leave and keep my identity unknown. That is my plan, unless you intervene."

Bartholomew replied, "Yes, that could work. But it will be very hard to do, especially if you go to Holtsclaw Abbey. Which, by the way, I continue to highly recommend. The mages there, some of them anyway, are very sensitive to *gift* in others. They may not see you as a master-mage yet. But they will certainly sense your exceptional power. Do you mind if I ask you a few questions?'

"No. If I can answer them, I will."

"A master-mage, if you are one, can *pull* or *absorb* the gift of others. Or so say the myths. Is it true? You can pull *gift* as well as push it from yourself? Pushing *gift* is how we use *it*. And why we are limited to the power we naturally possess."

Marcus pondered his reply. This was the one thing that mages would fear more than anything else, the inability of casting *gift* against him. Any attempt to do so would merely make him stronger at the expense of the mage who cast. His grandfather knew this was so. But Marcus was concerned he had not comprehended fully its terrible potential. But it seemed too late, now, to lie about it. "Yes, you are right. And not just from other mages, but from all living things. And even from the great river of *gift* flowing through the earth, under the right conditions. But I have to be careful. If I pull too much from something living, I can take away its very life."

Bartholomew hung his head. "Saul, this we must take to our

graves." He turning to Marcus. "And you must swear that you will never seek dominion or power over others. For as your great namesake discovered, and yes, I know the old stories, the fear of what you *might* do could bring about your downfall. Promise you will always use your *gift* for peace."

"That I can and so promise. I have no ambition for power or wealth."

Saul spoke in a low voice. "May *fata* spare us if you ever do."

Bartholomew concurred. "Amen to that. Now, there is one thing you must do, which neither I nor your grandfather is now capable. You must destroy Sinifir."

"And how do you propose I do that?"

"You must confront him, antagonize him into attacking you, then pull his power away, his very life if possible. With his strength in *mind-gift*, he can only be destroyed by using his own power against him. You have upset his plans that have been long in preparing. He will confront you before he makes other plans. Of that you can be sure."

Saul gave a weary sigh. "It's late. We will speak of this more, tomorrow." With that they left the ballroom and returned to their quarters.

Marcus was tired, but too deep in thought to sleep. *Destroy Sinifir.* He knew the dark mage held no power over him, but not so for others. And he was worried for his three friends. Sinifir might hesitate to confront him. If so, he would act quickly, in retaliation, and to guarantee their silence. *Time.* If only he had enough time to find his friends and protect them. He remembered the words of Kentuck. *Tiemp cannot be denied. Manipulated perhaps a little. But not denied. In the end it takes us all.* What did he mean, *could be manipulated?* He had tried every possible combination of doing so, casting *tiemp* every way he could imagine. All to no effect. He got up and retrieved Kentuck's dictionary from the corner chest. He opened it to *tiemp,* as he had done so many times before.

Such ability, to manipulate time, comes to us by myth more than fact. However, like so many myths, it could well be based in truth. It seems consistent, given other myths of ancient mages who could appear and disappear at will. By manipulating time, or their presence within it, this seemingly impossible ability would be child's play. I have pondered this much, and believe this manipulation of tiemp *is indeed possible by a mage with appropriate gift. Such a mage, such power in gift, must be rare indeed. For there is nothing within known records that confirms such an ability.*

Marcus read this cryptic statement several more times. His mind finally caught on the short phrase 'or their presence within it'. Up to now he had been trying to cast *tiemp*. But time could not be manipulated. Not if it were flowing constantly. That's what his grandfather had said. *Change how time flows? That's why we called him Kentuck the Crazy. He was always spouting off foolish things like that.* But what if both were right? If time could not be changed, could he change how he reacted *within* time? If he could somehow insert or remove *himself* into the flow of time, and manipulate events that way? But how does one cast *himself?* He was left pondering this as he drifted off to sleep.

Marcus arose very early, had a quick morning meal, and hurried off to the military training area. Following a hunch, he looked for a note from his friends. There was one, from Greta. It had been written the night before.

Sad news, my friend Marcus. When we refused to participate in the assassinations, Captain Morris commanded Louton to destroy us. He seized Ivan before we could intervene, and broke his neck. But Ivan was able to get one blow in, a fatal blade to Louton's reins. Captain Morris seized a cross-bow and shot Thomas in the throat before he could move to Ivan's defense. I have broken my vow to never take another life, for I cast my dagger at Captain Morris, striking him dear to the heart. I have left the dead where they fell. It has taken me some time to write this and I fear discovery, for guardsmen are searching everywhere for us. I am sure the bodies will soon be discovered. I will return here one last time for your final message, should you choose to send one. Beyond that, there is nothing more for me to do here. Please do not search after me. As always, I survive, but forever more with the shame of a broken vow. Please do not think poorly of me in this. I did it only for my friends. Your forever friend, Greta

Marcus wiped the tears from his eyes. He was in part responsible for their deaths. They had wanted to withdraw but he had argued against it. *Stay and do what you can.* They had stayed. They had died. And there had been precious little they could do to stop Sinifir's evil plans. Not knowing what else to do, Marcus ported to Katrina's quarters. He found her pacing, her door locked with a chair leaned against the handle to keep it secure. She rushed into his arms.

"Oh cousin. Have you heard? They found Captain Morris dead, and the remaining assassins as well. All dead. Sinifir and Stephen are beside themselves. But in a way, they also seem relieved, as there are no more tongues to betray them."

"There is one more remaining, but she is gone, beyond their reach. You know that two of those who died were my friends, right?"

"Yes, that's what you said to the guards-men. 'Spare them. They have been trying to stop this'. I'm sorry for your loss. They were close friends?"

"Closest friends I have ever had. Perhaps that isn't much," he sad sadly, tears pooling at the corner of his eyes. "But they were also the *only* friends I have ever had. Except for you, of course. This *gift* I possess? It forces me to remain apart from others. It's time like this I truly wish to be rid of it."

"She put her arms around his waist and pulled him close. No, don't ever say that, Marcus. This *gift* you have. It gives you the power to do great things, good things. You must never rue the power to do good." She stroked his cheeks, dried his tears. "What is our plan to destroy Sinifir?"

"Our plan?"

She gave him a determined look. "Yes. And to destroy Stephen as well. Else he will eventually destroy me. He continues to make that clear in his relentless pacing and raves."

Their conversation was disrupted by the sound of fighting in the residential corridor beyond her doors. They rushed through the parlor, casting chairs aside in their haste, and burst into the hallway. Two guards-men were lying still, another was down on a knee, desperately holding his entrails in place. His abdomen lay open from groin to navel. He, too, would soon be dead. "You must hurry," he gasped. "The Mage is attacking the Crown Prince." With that, he garbled something more, then keeled over in shock and pain. And death.

Marcus raced to the door of the Crown Prince's quarters. There was a clash of fighting, blade against blade. Marcus tried the door. It was locked, from within. Using all his strength, he smashed a shoulder against it. To no avail. The royal quarters had been securely built. Focusing *gift*, he cast a bolt of flame, fo-see-AH, at the lock. It shattered in a blast of embers. Smoke billowed into the hallway. The door, partly blasted from its hinges, fell open.

Marcus captured the image in an instant. Sinifir stood over the Crown Prince, his blade poised to fall in what would surely be a fatal thrust. Marcus was struck with sudden understanding. Crazy Kentuck had provided the clue. And his grandfather had also been right. Time could not be stopped. But he could control *his* passage through it. He imagined himself, his entire self, and cast his whole being into *tiemp*. Everything simply *stopped*. The expression on Sinifir's face was frozen in a visage of pure hate. His long-blade was suspended, unmoving. Marcus saw that he was wielding his grandfather's old-steel mage-blade. It was a blade that only the current Lord High-mage was entitled to wear. He sadly understood that Crown Prince Jared was to be Sinifir's second victim that day. Or counting the three guards lying lifeless in the hallway, his fifth.

With some difficulty, Marcus found that he could move in this time-frozen environment. He made his way to Sinifir and withdrew the mage-blade from his grasp. He unfastened the belt and sheath from his waist and secured them around his own. He wiped the blood, probably some of it his grandfather' own, on Sinifir's dark robe. He returned the blade in its sheath. With difficulty, he dragged the Crown Prince across the floor and into the hall. He then re-entered the quarters and levered the door back into place as best he could. Hinges were broken, so it did not hang evenly. The time had come to deal with Sinifir.

Marcus stood three paces from the unmoving and disarmed dark mage. Bracing himself, he pulled his *being* back from *tiemp*. Time restored itself. The shock on Sinifir's face was palpable. He looked down to the missing Crown Prince. He looked at his empty hands. He then looked at Marcus. Confusion gave way to unbridled hate. Beyond the hate, Marcus' mind-touch revealed a mage, a dark mage, driven to insanity by an unfettered but frustrated ambition for power. Consequences were no longer a concern.

There was no need to goad Sinifir into an attack. He stretched forth both hands and invoked some word of power that was foreign to Marcus. He flinched with the mental blow of viciously cast mind-power. Sinifir smiled. "Weak, just like your sniveling grandfather. And I'm going to do to you what I did to him. He cried like a baby by the time I was through with him. Kept going on and on about not wanting to die, that he still had work to do. He *begged* for his life. Hear me? *Begged*. It was utterly disgusting to see a *Lord High-mage* begging for his life. And it was a joy to see him die, writhing in pain. Now it's *your* turn, you meddling boy. Take *this!*"

Marcus felt another surge of *mind-gift*, stronger than the first.

But instead of flinching, or reacting in any other way, he simple pulled it in. Welcomed it! He opened his own reservoirs of *gift* to receive it, much as he had done with *gift-flow* during a new moon surge. Sinifir tried again and again to destroy him. Marcus smiled at each attempt. It finally dawned on Sinifir that his mind-power was having no effect. He tried to withdraw. Marcus held him fast. The *gift* force was flowing faster now, ever faster. Like water running downhill. There was alarm, then panic, fear written on Sinifir's face. "No. No. This is not possible. Let me go. Let me GO." Marcus refused, continuing to hold him fast by the flow of *gift*.

Marcus could tell when Sinifir's *gift* power was fully depleted. There was a sudden change in the flavor? texture? of the *gift* that he was withdrawing. Memories began to emerge as the *gift*-flow finally reached Sinifir's life-force. Marcus saw the many evils he had schemed. There were thefts and murders, all in the pursuit of power and wealth. He saw the caches of gold and silver Sinifir had secreted here in the castle. He saw seductions, blackmails and other intrigues. Enough to cause him nausea. But release Sinifir? He did not. The memories stretched further and further back in time, to his wanderings before Iber, And eventually to his training in the dark mage school in the deserts of Illium. To when he had first emerged as a mind-mage. Then he was a child, an infant. Marcus felt a faint snap, and there was nothing left to absorb. Sinifir was gone, never to return. His life force had been extinguished. The lifeless body wilted to the floor. Marcus went to his knees and his stomach voided.

When his gorge had finally ended, Marcus looked up to see the Crown Prince looking down at him. "You survive." It was said as a simple statement of fact. "And Sinifir does not."

Marcus nodded, not speaking.

"I know not the ways of mages, the powers you wield. Nor do I want to know them." There was a pause. "I am truly sorry about your grandfather. Sinifir boasted of his death as we fought. I see you have retrieved your family blade."

Marcus nodded again. "It was a desecration to see him wear it."

"Yes. Sinifir did much evil here. Again, I won't ask how you defeated him, I'm only glad that he is gone. Few will mourn him, perhaps the King. Certainly my son, Prince Stephen. We are without a Lord High-mage. Will you want to fill your grandfather's place? It is your right, by tradition."

"I don't know. But I doubt it. Certainly not for some turns, at least. It is best you make other plans."

"I understand. I leave you to your grieving." He departed, giving the guards the command to leave the room untouched until further notice. His place was taken by Katrina. She knelt down in front of him, pulling his face into her hands. She turned his head up to look into his eyes and spoke with great emotion. "I know this is a hard time, but it is *done*. Whatever the cost, your grandfather wanted Iber to survive. He protected us to the very end. He will be remembered, as will you. She put her arms around his neck, buried her face in his neck and wept. She did not weep alone.

The King was furious and refused to believe Sinifir had been responsible for Saul's death. *I knew him well. He was incapable of such an act.* And in denying this, he was even more angry with Marcus, who had taken the dark mage's life. The Crown Prince worked hard on Marcus' behalf. He finally persuaded the King to suspend any action against him until the facts were fully known. Sinifir's death was a certainty. Too many had seen the corpse for it to be denied.

Marcus had taken careful note of the Crown Prince's quarters, and had no problem porting. The guards posted outside the door, of course, were completely unaware. He picked up the strangely limp body of Sinifir and ported to the distant glade beyond Claron Falls. Closing the portal, he dumped the body next to the grave-like depression he had created turnings before. A sudden thought came to him, one sure to create confusion and fear. Quickly, he stripped Sinifir of his clothing, bundling and wrapping them in his black cape. In doing so Marcus found three things of interest: a pair of finely engraved black daggers of that same unknown metal, a coin purse of considerable weight, and within the purse, a deep-red stone the size and shape of an early-bird's egg. The daggers he placed in his belt, the coin purse in a pocket of his own cape. He rolled the now-nude body into the depression and drew earth upon it, obscuring it completely. *"From earth we all come, to earth we all go. In the end time takes us all."* Marcus paused in his eulogy. *"For you, Sinifir, there will be no burial with honors, only an unmarked and forgotten grave. And your soul, Sinifir, may it rot in hell."* With that he spit on the grave, turned, and ported back to the quarters of the Crown Prince. There he unbundled the clothing and spread it out on the floor in the location and general position of the corpse. His last act was to place Sinifir socks within the ornate boots he had worn. No one had entered the rooms during the time it had taken Marcus to dispose of Sinifir's remains, posted guards willing to so affirm. . Marcus gave it all a final look-over. He was done. Satisfied, he ported to his quarters, leaving only a great mystery in his wake.

Marcus placed the two black-metal daggers in the corner chest and opened Sinifir's purse. It was heavy. He counted a hand and two coppers, eight silvers, and a single gold crown. Together they were worth a full fist of silvers. All in all, Sinifir had carried a veritable fortune. *No surprise,*thought Marcus. *Not for a man obsessed with wealth.* Marcus returned the coin to the purse and placed it in the chest next to the black daggers.

The great mystery of Sinifir's disappearance was kept quiet. Rumors circulated of course. They became more bizarre with each retelling. His grandfather's funeral was a different matter. Saul was honored in death befitting a Lord High-mage and brother-in-law to the King. He was laid to rest next to his beloved Susannah. A multitude of mourners looked on in grief. The Caledonian Envoy and Bartholomew remained three additional days to attend the funeral and to witness a return of the Kingdom to stability. They hoped for the dismissal of Sinifir's army of aggression. But in this they were disappointed.

Bartholomew and Marcus had had several opportunities to share confidences. Marcus confirmed the manner of Sinifir's death He made no mention of his involvement in the disappearance of his body. Bartholomew had simply nodded, saying nothing. But the way he looked at Marcus made it clear he knew who was responsible. Somehow.

On the day following the funeral, Marcus was summoned to the quarters of the Crown Prince. "Marcus, the King continues to deny Sinifir's role in the death of your grandfather. He insists it was by the hand of a yet unknown assassin. But of your involvement in Sinifir's death, there is no question. He is therefore trying to decide what to do. Should he have you hung? Or banished from the Kingdom. In the first, you must prepare to flee at a moment's notice. In the second, you must prepare to flee, with perhaps several *moments* of notice. Not much difference, eh?"

"Thank you. I guess I'll be... preparing to flee. But I have a particular request."

"If I can grant it, I will."

"My grandfather and Mage Bartholomew, High-mages both, felt strongly I should attend a distant mage academy. Holtsclaw Abbey. It is far away, no less than two hand-fists across the mainland. I would go there and learn to control my *gift* more completely and safely. You have seen what I am capable of doing. They and I think it best to see its power developed further, under the supervision of stronger mages than myself."

"A wise precaution. Since you will be leaving in any case, I see no problem. You certainly don't need my permission. So what exactly is your request?"

"It is a matter of coin, sir. The cost of the school must be met in advance. It is one gold crown per turning. For the full four turns it would amount to a full hand and six crowns."

"A hand and six crowns? You must be mad, Marcus, if you expect such from the royal treasury! Sinifir's fake war preparations have left the Kingdom's treasury close to empty. It is all we can do to meet expenses from one seven-day to the next. So, the answer is *no*. I would be happy to write a letter of introduction, even a recommendation. But no way would I be able to help with expenses. Certainly not of that magnitude."

Marcus nodded in disappointed acknowledgement. "I understand. You did recover the coin secreted by Sinifir, yes?"

"Yes, thanks to your help. It is much appreciated. It was considerable, as you know. Without it, we might not be meeting expenses even today. Do you have enough to get by? You will need kit for travel, if you plan on leaving soon. Fourth turning will soon be upon us. I could personally give you, say, a full hand of silvers. Perhaps as many as a full hand five, though that would be a stretch."

"Thank you, Crown Prince. No, I won't need anything before I depart. Grandfather had some coin saved, silvers and coppers. Probably a two hand of silver. A two-hand should be more than enough to get me on my way. I'm going to begin preparations immediately. As you say, I'll have to flee in any case."

Marcus returned to his quarters. Everything was strangely quiet and empty without his grandfather's presence. He took careful thought to his traveling requirements. He would take the old-steel long-blade that had been in his family for four-hand generations. And of course, the two short-blades given him by Master Kelson. He would carry his bo with its attached sling. It would be equally effective as a cross-bow and of similar range and accuracy. He would forego a long-bow. Beyond weapons, he would take his copy of the mage chronicles and Kentuck's dictionary. There was little else to take of a personal nature, leaving the rest of his pack to traveling essentials. The time camping with his grandfather, and the many days and nights in the field with siege weaponry, provided good training for his travel. There was the customary cooking pot, eating and cleaning utensils, a variety of spices and herbs, and a few hygiene supplies. For clothing he had to purchase additional small-clothes, several warm under-shirts and under-leggings, several wool sweaters and a warm snow- hood. And gloves, several warm pairs. A tent and ground cloth were already in his possession. He stretched himself out on his bed and mentally went through his trip. He imagined walking and camping in a diversity of conditions. *Boots!* He had to think carefully about foot-ware. Surely the outfitter could advise in that regard. At last, he slept.

The next morning he made his way through the west gate of the castle, to the now-familiar outfitter's store. The owner recognized him. "Sorry about your grandfather. He was a good man. How may I help you this morning?"

"Thank you for remembering him. We all miss him greatly. As for helping me, with him gone, I am looking at a long journey. Possibly soon. If you were undertaking such a journey, what would you require? I have some things. But I certainly need to purchase others."

"Well, let me see. You will be afoot, I gather? If so, the first thing you need is a *good* pack. And by good, I mean a *really* good one. Having a lot to carry will wear you out quickly if you cannot carry it comfortably, and conveniently. You will be packing and unpacking constantly. A good pack will make that both simple and quick. Do you have a pack?"

"Yes, but it is more geared for light travel, perhaps a day or so. What else will I need?"

After a time of discussion and rummaging through the store,

Marcus emerged with a *good* pack, a better tent and ground-cloth (two), a cooking pan to go with his pot, better water flagons (two), boots (two pair), wool socks (three pair), small clothes, leather breeches (one pair), wool breeches (one pair), and so on. He also had a bundle of spices, dried meat, and salt. In total, it came to almost three silvers. Marcus gave the merchant the full three, grateful for his help. Together they loaded the pack. It was nearly full. He calculated there would be just enough room at the bottom for the manuscripts he intended to carry, the pot, and a few other supplies he already had in his possession. It was heavy. But fortunately, not so heavy that Marcus would struggle unnecessarily. He returned to his quarters. It was mid-day.

CHAPTER

SIXTEEN

Having little else to do, Marcus ported to Katrina's quarters. He arrived to find her bruised and battered. "What..."

She held up her hand and spoke through a split lip. "Stephen. Who else?"

" Did he..."

"*Use* me? No, but he will be back. When his own lip has healed a bit. I gave as well as I got."

"Does your father, the Crown Prince, know of this... this *violation?*"

"Not yet, but he will, As soon as he returns from his meetings with the King. I've sent word through one of the castle staff."

"And Stephen knows this? That your father is coming?"

"Probably yes, by now. Castle staffers have been talking. He's sure to have overheard. Marcus, would you consider staying here until my father comes? I think he will deal harshly with Stephen. And Stephen might want to exact his revenge before hand."

Marcus readily agreed. They spoke for some time. Marcus told her about the choices he faced and the preparations he had made. He told her about Holtsclaw Abbey, the distance he would have to travel to get there, and the uncertainty of paying tuition. He had some ideas in that regard, he told her. But left it vague. *Because they were vague.* At last, there was a knock at the door. She rose, answered, and admitted her father to the room. Marcus rose in respect.

Crown Prince Jared gave Marcus a suspicious eye. "You are here, in my daughter's quarters, without a chaperone?"

"Father, it is *Cousin* Marcus. And I invited him here because I feared Stephen. Nothing inappropriate has happened between us. And he came discretely."

"All right," the Crown Prince replied, still with a bit of suspicion in his voice. "And you look terrible. Wait here, while I go and fetch Stephen. I've had enough of his ill treatment of you. And others."

"Others?" asked Katrina.

He waved his hand as he left the room. "Not of your concern. Wait here."

Several moments passed. The door finally slammed open and Stephen stumbled into the room. He was followed by a very angry father. Marcus acknowledge quietly to himself. *Katrina certainly gave as much as she received.* Stephen had a black eye, a split and swollen lower lip, and scratches across his face.

"Now son, explain yourself. I rather doubt she initiated this little fracas."

Stephen stood sullenly silent, refusing to answer. Suddenly, he spun, stabbing a blade into his father's chest. The Crown Prince collapsed with a gurgle, blood pouring from the wound. There was shock and disbelief in his eyes. In an instant a blade hissed through the air and impaled itself in Stephen's throat. He collapsed without a sound, falling next to his father. All of this passed in a flash before Marcus' eyes. The blade had come from Katrina.

"Marcus, please, you must help my father!"

Marcus cast himself down to kneel next to the Crown Prince. He carefully withdrew the blade. It had perforated a lung, which was quickly filling with blood. Marcus followed the blade's path, closing the wound as he did so. Though deep, the blade had not severed anything additional. He was at a loss how to void the lung, but at least the hemorrhaging had ceased. He sat back. "Katrina, I've done what I can. It will be up to the healer-mages to treat him further. I believe he is out of immediate danger."

A muffled "thank you, Marcus, for a second time" came from the Crown Prince. "And Stephen?"

"I killed him, father. I put a blade through his throat."

Her father groaned. "Not good, my daughter. For all his faults, he was my heir and his grandfather's favorite. The penalty for killing a royal is... death."

"She didn't kill him. I did." Marcus surprised himself with his words. "I am facing death or banishment in any case. You cannot lose them both. It would leave the kingdom, your kingdom, without an heir. And we both know she is more worthy to take your place than Stephen ever would have been."

The Crown Prince looked at Katrina, nodded, and coughed blood. He struggled to speak. "He is right, Katrina. We must agree. It was he who did this. In my defense, yes, but still it was he who has taken Stephen's worthless life."

"No! I won't let that happen to him. *I* did it. And I'm not sorry. I will take whatever..."

Marcus put a hand over her mouth. He spoke in a whisper. "Not so loud. Your father is right. This is the way it *has to be*. And we take this secret to our graves. Now, what is first? We need to hide Stephen's body. At least for as long as it takes me to quit the city. When he is out of the way, we get the Crown Prince to the health-mages. If anyone asks, tell them Stephen stabbed you, Crown Prince. And I reacted in response. Then fled. At least the first and last parts are true. Now, Katrina, help me move his body to your bedroom. They will be reluctant to look there. At least for a while." Katrina went to the outside corridor and summoned a member of the castle staff. "Hurry, the Crown Prince lies gravely injured, Summon health-mages, immediately. Quickly!" The staffer sprinted off down the hall in search of help.

Marcus told the Crown Prince to brace himself for yet another surprise. A portal opened to Marcus' quarters, and he walked through. The portal closed behind him.

"What? How?

"It's a portal, father. More mage ability. Marcus has come here often in the same way, to exchange information on Stephen and Sinifir. What they did not know is that their conversations were easily overheard between our walls. Back near the comfort area." She tried to cheer her father. "And don't worry, Marcus has never laid a hand on me. Though I must confess, the thought of it has pleasantly passed through my mind from time to time."

Crown Prince chuckled, then coughed more blood. "You two. I didn't think there could be any greater surprise than seeing your blade-dance. Wasn't I..." He coughed again, more blood. "Wasn't I ever wrong! Marcus told his grandfather you had emerged with battle-gift. And he told me. Is this so?"

"So thinks Marcus. It would explain a lot of things, Father."

Imagine having a battle-mage as a queen of Iber. That's a day to live for!"

Two health mages rushed into the room. "Oh my, is he bleeding out! Let us at him!"

"He's no longer bleedin. But his one lung is filled with blood."

The two mages gave each other a puzzled look and shrugged. They lifted the Crown Prince onto a stretcher, which had just arrived on the shoulders of two other members of the castle staff. They departed quickly, leaving Katrina alone, wondering what to do next. Wondering what would happen to her. And wondering what would happen to Marcus. Emotion and distress overcame her. She sat on the sofa, placed her face in her hands, and began to cry.

Marcus hurriedly began to pack. Earlier, he had mentally gone through the process several times. Within a brief time he was ready to leave. There was but two things left to do. He sat at his desk and wrote. When finished, he shouldered his pack and weapons, picked up the copper box wrapped in its two layers of sealskin, and ported back to Katrina's room. Fortunately, she was still alone. Her tears had dried.

"Marcus? You should be gone by now..."

"Yes, and I will be leaving in a moment or two. There is something I want you to have. For over four-hand generations, each Lord High-mage has kept a record of the proceedings of Iber during his lifetime. They wrote only one page, each. The writing is small. The oldest of pages, the first hand and five generations, are written in *Kult*. The remainder are in our own language. The pages are very old, the oldest over a hand and two fist turns. I leave them in your care, as they are the history of *your* kingdom. The one you will someday rule. Read what you can. There is much wisdom in history, in *this* history. You will need it to rule wisely. I have made a copy. This is the original. Now, I go. If I survive and can port this far, I will return from time to time to check on you. Perhaps someday to become your Lord High-mage. In the meantime, I have asked a friend to look after you. She will identify herself, if she chooses to serve, as 'Greta. A friend of Marcus'. You can trust your life to her." He bent down, pulled her close, and gently kissed her lips, careful to avoid her injury. "Oh, for the things that might have been!"

She kissed him in return, with little regard for whatever pain it caused. "Oh yes. For all the things that might have been. And still might be? Good-bye, dear cousin. I love you."

"And I love you too." He shrugged. "And it's *second* cousin."
With that he turned and ported away to the military complex. He
invoked *tiemp* and made his way to the place where messages had
been passed so many times before. He left his note for Greta,
hoping she would think to look one last time. As she had promised
she would.

Greta my friend. And that is a title I have given but to a few. I
speak for many in saying we hold no regret for your vow breaking.
Nor do we think less of you for doing so. There is no greater gift than
that which we give to protect the ones we love. With that, I have but
one final request. I leave it to you to act on it or not. There is one I
leave behind, one I dearly love. It may well be that I will not live to
see her again. She is Princess Katrina. Whatever you might do to
keep her safe would be the greatest gift for which I could ever hope.
In time she will rule Iber. I believe she will become one of the great
queens Iber has ever seen, or will ever see. For the love of Iber, may
she live to fulfill her destiny. If you wish to serve her, simply identify
yourself as Greta, a friend of Marcus. She will understand. I have
told her, as I truly believe, that she can trust her life to your care.
Your always friend, Marcus.

Marcus stood on a hill-top a hand of leagues east of Alexa. He had
ported there from the castle, from the military complex. It was a
place he knew well, a place where he had spent much time during
his training with siege weapons. They would all be looking for him
on the road to Sudsport. So he would take the harsh northern route,
rarely traveled, that led to Norsport. With third turning ending and
fourth turning coming in its wake, it would be a hard trip. And he
was now a fugitive with a bounty on his head. He turned his back
on the city, and took his first steps east, into the unknown.

CHAPTER SIXTEEN

End of Book One

To be continued

SNEEK PEAK OF FUGITIVE

MASTER MAGE CHRONICLES BOOK TWO

Marcus was ten leagues east of Alexa and one league north of the trade route to Sudsport. He had ported to the training area for siege weapons, though no training was scheduled for this late in the third turning. Foothills, giving way closely to mountains, provided ample ammunition for trebuchet and catapult. It was an area he knew very well, having camped there a full turning.

Marcus had decided to flee the Kingdom of Iber via Nordsport. Those who went on foot, as he, would have a difficult passage over a harsh and difficult landscapes of mountains, rivers and cliff. And in late third turning, no one would be making the attempt. He would have to follow the trade route for several days before the Nordsport path diverged to the north at the River Aro. He would be traveling alone beyond. But for now he would need to be very careful, as the trade route was well traveled. There really wasn't an alternative. The surrounding countryside was a patchwork of small holdings, each separated from its neighbors by hedgerows and ditches. And holdings were home to guard dogs.

Except for an occasional barking, Marcus was able to make his way soundlessly to the trade route without incident. He secreted himself in a line of low bushes and waited for nightfall. There was a waxing half-moon that gave him sufficient light to travel safely. Unlike Alexa, the surrounds were rural with little night-life. He was grateful for the new pack. His load, though heavy, rested comfortably on his shoulders.

He entered the trade road and turned east, away from Alexa, and began a steady pace. He kept to the shadowed side. The road itself was paved, the pavers rough-hewn but worn reasonable smooth by the passage of time and countless wagons, hooves and feet. It was wide enough for the passage of two wagons. Two pairs of faint grooves in the stone were clearly visible in the moonlight. Traffic itself was sparse. There was no foot traffic and he encountered only a few merchants going about their business. The were slumped in wagon seats and nodding in half-awareness as draft animals wound their relentless way to or from a distant stall. Marcus withdrew to a shadowed retreat as they passed him by. When he overtook a wagon, which only happened twice, he invoked *tiemp* and hurried ahead, not rejoining normal time until well in advance. Two things struck him about moving through time. First, it was utterly and totally silent. And second, it took more effort to move. The air was *thick*, and each time he returned to normal time after a long foray, he found himself sweating and aching of leg muscle.

The sky began to lighten and Marcus searched for a place to hide. He had been traveling in darkness since the mid-night setting of the moon. To his dismay, the dawning revealed nothing but an endless vista of pastures and fields. He kept walking, fearing discovery. There was a field to his right with ricks of hay, each stacked around a central pole. He climbed through the low hedgerow, walked carefully to the row farthest from the highway, and buried himself in a corner rick. Inside it was dark. The hay was freshly-cut and had a rich smell of earth and leaf, not entirely unpleasant. The ground was cool and moist. Marcus finally worked his ground cloth free, grateful for the advice to keep it near the top. He pressed out a space to sit and ate some dried meat and part of a loaf of bread. He then drank deeply from his flagon of water, rolled up in a blanket, and quickly fell asleep.

In was late morning. Marcus was awakened from his slumber by the approaching sound of voices. There were a few moments of disorientation as he struggled to remember where he was and how he had gotten there. The sounds came from his left. He carefully parted the hay and saw, to his chagrin, an older man and two younger, probably his sons. They wielded large wooden pitching forks, with which they had begun loading the hay, rick-by-rick, onto a large flat wagon pulled by a pair of oxen. Fortunately, they had entered the field from the trade route, through a break in the hedgerow Marcus had overlooked in the dawn's early light.

The three men made quick work of the first rick. There was space on the wagon for many more. Marcus tried to estimate how long it would take them to reach his location. His only 'plan', if it could be called such, was to wait as long as possible, invoke *tiemp*, and leave the field unnoticed. The problem, of course, was that he had no place to go. Time seemed to pass slowly. Mid-day came and went. The farmers paused for a meal. By late afternoon they were down to the last row. Marcus was glad he had chosen to obscure himself at the further-most corner of the field. The men were close enough to be clearly heard.

"Call it a day, boys," the father said. "The wagon's full. Let's take this load back to the barn and get it unloaded. We'll finish the rest of these in the morning."

With a sigh of relief, Marcus fell back to lie again on the earth. "*Fata* be blessed!" He was safe.

Again, Marcus began his travels well after sunset. The moon was not quite as high in the sky as the night before, meaning there would be an extra period of moonlight to illuminate his way. By early morning he was favored by occasional patches of low forest in damp, boggy areas unsuitable, he assumed, for farming. He selected a copse somewhat denser than others and went as deeply as he felt necessary to remain hidden. He found a camping spot in a small open area that was reasonable dry. There was an abundance of kindling. He gathered twigs and cast a small, smokeless flame. He unpacked his cooking pots and prepared and ate a hot meal. It was his first in a two-day. He finished with a bowl of fresh berries that grew around him in abundance. His spirits lifted.

The day passed uneventfully. He slept, but fitfully, then arose and prepared another hot meal. Shortly before night-fall he retraced his path to the highway and resumed his travel. One more day, perhaps a day and a half, and he would be at the great stone *Bridge of Aro*. Its name derived from the mighty river it spanned. He thought about increasing his pace, but then thought *to what end?* He would have to wait until nightfall in any case. And though he had rested adequately enough, the leagues of bearing a heavy pack had left him tired and sore.

The weather, which had been favorable, now turned against him. It began with a breeze, strengthening into a stiff wind. Light rain, then a heavier rain, began to fall. Fortunately for Marcus, the storm was sweeping down from the mountains to the west, at his back. He paused under a spreading big-leaf tree and rummaged through his pack for the water-proof cape he had recently purchased. Although it was stiff, having never been worn, it kept him dry down to his knees. Unfortunately, it provided no protection below. The temperature began to fall. By dawn his feet were cold, and this in turn seemed to chill the rest of his body. He spent the day in the depths of another copse of trees, huddled around a small burn-pit. Marcus had tried casting flame, or heat, into his feet and legs. But to no avail. His capacity to absorb *gift* apparently applied to his own, as well. Rather than having its desired effect, his efforts simply returned power to him as quickly as it was cast. A bit disappointing, that.

It was a most unpleasant night of struggling over cold stone with wet stocking and boot. Well before dawn he found himself approaching the River Aro. Its muffled roar of rushing water clearly sounded in the distance. Foot and wagon traffic increased as morning came, as there was a substantial village, Aro, of course, at the river crossing. Just beyond, on the east side of the river, would be the turn-off to Nordsport. That would be his objective for the following night. And then to be well away from the trade-route he had been perilously following the last two-day. Or was it a three-day? Truthfully, Marcus had lost count, portending badly for a long trip just in its beginning.

Fortunately, the harsh weather relented. A genuine forest grew along the river's path, extending to the rising hills beyond. Darkness fell and Marcus walked cautiously over the stone bridge, marveling at its height and sturdy construction. The Aro was far below. Its raging flow was impressive. Even so, he could imagine it being so much greater during the spring run-off.

Reaching the other side of the bridge, he slipped into the shadows of what appeared to be the largest structure in the village. It was the only building he could see with a hanging lamp. It swung lazily over a large title board, proclaimed it to be, simply, *The Inn at Aro*. The smell of hot meat was enticing. The prospects of a warm flame, dry clothes and a soft bed, overwhelming. He considered his options and their risks. Logic told him to keep going without pause. But then, he was tired, hungry, and in need of a bath. His many discomforts argued with logic. Here, in Aro, a full two-day from Alexa, he should still be reasonably unknown? At the least, he could quietly enter, find a private, dark corner, and order a hot meal? Ignoring the warnings screaming through his head, he circled the inn to the rear and carefully hid his pack. Cautiously, he returned to the front and entered. He was immediately assaulted by the warmth of a roaring flame and the aroma of cooking meat.

A young serving girl approached. "Sir?"

"A quiet table for a weary traveler, please. Weak-mead and food?"

"Of course. Three coppers for the lot. Follow me."

Three coppers were much for a meal, but Marcus did not argue. He reached the table and sat wearily. As requested, it was in a dimly lit corner near the kitchen entrance. Marcus pressed the three coppers into the server's open hand. She moved to the bar and dropped the coppers into a locked box on the lower shelf next to the kegs of mead. She then slipped a hand into the pocket of her loose apron and smiled. Curious, Marcus extended mind-touch. *Two for the master, one for me!* A moment later she returned with a flagon of warm weak-mead. Mead was a honey-based drink and could be strongly brewed. Weak-mead, as he had ordered, wasn't much more than sweetened water. He drank deeply, paused, then drank again, draining the large flagon.

"More, sir? Your food will be right out. It is venison, tonight. One of the local hunters brought in a large stag early this afternoon. We are not often so fortunate."

Marcus nodded his approval and said nothing more. A few moments later, he was enjoying the venison. It was well cooked and heavily spiced, served with a side dish of tubers and greens. He was just finishing when the sound of horses and men could be heard approaching the inn. The doors were thrown open and two men, wearing capes emblazoned with the crest and regalia of the king's guard, strode boldly into the room. The serving maid was quick to greet them, bowing in deference.

"We come looking for a solitary traveler, young. Have you seen such? He is a dangerous criminal and there is a bounty on his head, dead or alive."

The maid, frightened, nodded her head. "Y-Y-Yes, we have such a traveler. H-H-He sits in yonder corner, by the kitchens." She pointed to the table where Marcus had been sitting. The table was vacant and cleared of utensils.

Made in the USA
Middletown, DE
05 June 2023

31850448R00128